How Steve Spurrier Brought Glory Home To Florida Football

By W.F. Buddy Martin

KENDALL/HUNT PUBLISHING COMPANY
4050 Westmark Drive P.O. Box 1840 Dubuque, Iowa 52004-1840

This edition has been printed directly from camera-ready copy.

ISBN 0-7872-1243-1

Printed in the United States of America
10 9 8 7 6 5 4 3 2 1

'We are all strong for old Florida,

<u>Down Where The Old Gators Play</u>
(Go Gators!)

In all kinds of weather,
We'll all stick together
For F-L-O-R-I-D-A!'

--*Song traditionally sung between third and fourth quarters of all Florida home football games*

In loving memory of

Margaret O'Quinn Martin Cannon

1902-1975

who asked so little
and gave so much

TABLE OF CONTENTS

I find the great thing in this world is not so much where we stand, as in what direction we are moving.

To reach the port of heaven, we must sail sometimes with the wind and sometimes against it--but we must sail, and not drift, nor lie at anchor.

---Oliver Wendell Holmes

FORWARD/BY FRANK FRANGIE

understanding Gator football

When I first learned of this book, I must admit: I rolled my eyes a bit. "Just what we need," I thought. "*ANOTHER* behind-the-scenes look at a season of University of Florida football!"

By my count, this made three books in four years. The others, authored by my friends Norm Carlson and Jeff Snook, were fine products. But did we need *ANOTHER*?

Then I learned a little about *Down Where The Old Gators Play.* About its mission, its intent. I already knew plenty about its author.

Buddy Martin, whose experience covers countless years and industries, has taken a great interest in the lives and careers of many young journalists and broadcasters. I am among those he has pointed in the right direction.

Through our friendship, I have come to understand Buddy's affinity for college football, and for the Gators. I understand how Florida football flows through his arteries, how its years of failures both frustrated and puzzled him; how its newfound glory has pleased him.

Apart from his spirituality and family, perhaps the only thing that matters more to him is integrity in his career and in the offerings he produces. All of which made this project a terrific fit.

It has played out accordingly. If you care about Florida Gator football--not just about one season, but its history--you will truly enjoy *Down Where The Old Gators Play.*

Moreover, if you have an interest in Southern college football anywhere, this book will pique your interest.

Because it is the tale, told through the eyes of a lifelong follower, of how passion for a college team can be encompassing, confounding and exhilarating.

Specifically, it explains how the 1994 season represents so much of Florida football history--a microcosm of almost 90 years of history in some ways; another breakthrough season in others.

It explains the pressures of being the Florida coach--past and present. And it delves deeply into the inner self of current coach Steve Spurrier, beloved and appreciated in many corners; despised and reviled in others.

Like Buddy Martin, I have followed Florida football for as long as I can remember and covered it as a reporter starting back in the mid-80s. As is the case with Buddy also, Steve Spurrier and I are friends and I am among those who like the coach a great deal.

Yet, after reading this book, I believe I understand Spurrier even better. I understand Florida football better. I even understand the passion of college football better.

Down Where The Old Gators Play does more than take you inside the locker room and behind the scenes.

It takes you inside the minds of coaches and quarterbacks, behind the tears of moms and dads and into the hearts of college football fans.

It is a wonderful product. I trust you will enjoy it thoroughly.

FRANK FRANGIE
WNZS Radio, *Florida SportsScene*
Jacksonville, Florida

INTRODUCTION

riding that hallelujah train

We are all pathfinders and, although we don't always know *where* we want to go, we often can sense when we're not on the right track. Sometimes we must head backwards or sideways in effort to advance forward. That's how Columbus sailed the ocean, Neil Armstrong walked on the moon and Steve Spurrier got back home to coach the Florida Gators.

Spurrier has always perceived life as one constant journey, which is why the aforementioned Oliver Wendell Holmes quote is one of his favorites. As Spurrier will attest, no matter where you're going, it seems, you've always got to leave home to get there.

And rarely are you afforded the chance to return back to that home, unless it's in a pine box. On that latter count, Steve Spurrier and this writer have been blessed.

It was a bizarre, circuitous route that brought Spurrier to Gainesville as a college player, took him away as a pro, brought him back as a young assistant and, finally, the journey back as the Prodigal Son of Florida football.

It was an unusual route, too, that brought me back to Ocala, Florida to begin working on this book in 1993 and, finally, the opportunity to sample a slice of life there again.

When you grow up in a small Southern town, you soon learn that if your daddy doesn't own the corner grocery store, the John Deere franchise or the Ford dealership, you are probably going to have to leave home someday.

Short of becoming a doctor or lawyer and coming back to practice on the local folk, the only remaining choice is to go chase rainbows someplace else. Yet from the day we first leave home, we begin working on our plot to someday return home to the nest.

Most of us are tied to an elastic umbilical cord which pulls us back upstream like a spawning salmon. Our quest is eternal, whereas the salmon only goes back once and then dies.

My journey has almost never stopped beckoning. Mostly by accident and only partially by design, I ventured out for a return to my roots as a writer--maybe to recapture some of my lost youth. And, at the same time, I hoped to experience the spiritual reawakening of Florida football.

Perhaps retracing my path in this fashion could also inspire new goals and boundaries for my writing.

There were so many questions to be answered about myself, as well as questions about the authenticity of Florida's No. 1 pre-season ranking, the operative word there being *pre-season.* As a lifelong Gator fan and a former University of Florida journalism student, I also had an emotional investment.

I had left Ocala the first time in 1963, on a path of journalistic endeavor to work for the *Nashville Tennessean* sports department for less money that I made at the *Ocala Star-Banner*.

Sometimes they make it hard, as well as expensive, to leave home, so six months later I returned to my old job in Florida.

Little did I realize that just 282 miles to the east of Nashville that spring, Steve Spurrier was about to start his real journey, heading south to Florida.

Spurrier was a hot-shot athlete from Science Hill High School in Johnson City who would someday drastically alter the course of college football in the state.

Had it not happened that Edwin Graves, brother of former Gator coach Ray Graves and postmaster in Knoxville, chanced to see Steve playing in a game, everything would be totally different in Gainesville today. And around the SEC..

I didn't know him Spurrier back then, but our paths would cross several times over the next 32 years.

Earlier that year in February of 1963 I had departed Ocala for Nashville with my wife and baby daughter aboard, pulling a U-Haul behind with every last possession to our name as cargo. For me, happiness was *not* looking back at Ocala, Florida in the rear view mirror of a nine-year-old Chevy.

Nor, apparently, was happiness watching your only son drive away with his wife and baby, knowing full well he wasn't prepared for the journey. For some reason I didn't quite grasp the tenderness of the moment as my mother, Margaret Martin, stood on the curb weeping, although it made me sad.

After all, I knew-- or *thought* I knew--I could always come back home. No wonder, then, I lasted only six months before I was afflicted with a serious case of homesickness.

In June of 1963 I returned home to Ocala and my old job as sports editor of the *Star-Banner.* That fall, Spurrier left Johnson City and became a Gator on the first leg of his mission to alter the course of Florida football.

The irony was that in the same year, just before my short stint in Tennessee, I had been a candidate for the job of University of Florida sports information director.

I finished runnerup to Norm Carlson, who's had the job ever since, except now he's been promoted to associate athletic director. Had Carlson not taken the job, my life would have been even more intertwined with Spurrier's.

Had that happened, who knows if Spurrier would have ever won the Heisman Trophy? Because Carlson had a big role in that. Instead, I got to write about the Golden Boy of Gator football while at the *Ocala Star-Banner, Florida Today,* later, *The St. Petersburg Times* and, of course, in this book.

In the process, I just kept coming back home and leaving.

Countless times over the next 32 years I would forsake Florida in search of success and then return home not knowing if I had found it or not.

My longest stretch away was nearly 12 years, first living in New York, then moving to my current Denver home 2,000 miles away in the Rocky Mountains.

The Florida sand was in my soul, not just my shoes, and I was determined to grasp a handful before it all sifted through the hour glass completely.

That's when life began to recycle itself.

Writing this book with Spurrier as a co-author seemed like a good idea to us both. The first thought about it occurred after I had just finished speaking to the Gainesville Quarterback Club in the spring of 1994, at which Spurrier agreed to introduce me.

What would it be like to go back home and live with your alma mater's football team for a season that held such great promise? At that time nobody knew just how big that promise would be, as the Florida Gators were about to be selected a consensus No. 1 in all the pre-season polls.

After several months of deliberation, Spurrier sent me a hand-written letter in July of that summer, reversing his field, saying he didn't want to take the time away from his team and coaching job to collaborate with me. He sensed what was at stake and the time constraints he would be under.

Though disappointed, I totally understood, but remained committed to my own conviction that I had sort of a stake in this team's whole venture. How were they going to win it all without me there to help?

I was intrigued by the team's prospects. And I felt some sense of pilgrimage about going back to live in my boyhood home for a while.

So I wrote Spurrier back, informing him I would write the book with or without him, but would appreciate his cooperation.

Our friendship was going to either be tested, or this was going to be a most enjoyable assignment.

In his return correspondence, Spurrier stated that this was a "fantastic idea."

It was well-meant when he promised: "I'll see you a whole lot this season and hopefully can add whatever I can to your book." Certainly a thoughtful gesture, but not a practical idea, because it didn't exactly work out that way.

Plainly, Spurrier's mission was to take Florida football to a new plateau, higher than even the places he had already taken it as either player or coach.

That sense of purpose is what keeps him totally focused on the job at hand, but it also makes him as elusive as catching lightning in a bottle. He was so pre-occupied at times that he became impossible to capture for more than a sound bite or two. At least until the season was over.

The '94 season was a roller-coaster ride fraught with player problems which kept Spurrier distracted. Neither of us ever dreamed that so many bizarre incidents would consume his time.

Not having the access to him that I had hoped for, I used the methods of observation, interviewing others and diligently gathering information wherever I could get it.

As the season was about to start, concerned that it might not live up to expectations, Spurrier asked me: "What will you do if we lose a game or two along the way?"

I explained to him that it wasn't going to be a case of merely chronicling the Gators' bid for a national championship.

"This book is about where Gator football has been and where it is going, about the culture surrounding Gator football--the players, the fans, the media--by somebody who has lived it his whole life," I explained to him. "Not just about a national championship."

OK, so maybe I *was* hoping they'd hit the lottery, too.

And it was a book very much about Steve Spurrier, the guy who had set Florida moving in a direction that even Oliver Wendell Holmes would like.

I spent many hours at practice, traveled five states and eight cities to cover 13 games and taped over 20 interviews with Spurrier in a group with other writers.

The only special favor I asked for--after the season was over--was the exclusivity of one final private, in-depth Spurrier interview in the spring of 1995, which he graciously granted.

And as an extra bonus, I was invited--as a friend--to his 50th birthday celebration where I joined a procession of about 18 speakers who would tag Spurrier that night with a little birthday greeting.

There was a six-week ride on The Hallelujah Train. The Gators did make a run for the national championship, albeit a short one. They lasted at No. 1 in the wire services polls for a week before slipping to No. 2 for one game, then enjoyed a five-week stint as the top-ranked college football team in the country. Florida's only other No. 1 ranking had lasted all of one week.

We all discovered that during those five weeks, at this new level, there was a far different kind of pressure, not to mention a few surprises. The biggest revelation for me was watching Spurrier work up close under the pressure of big-time college football.

I did not always know him, because there were sides of him I had never seen before:

Watching him battle the stress that goes with the intense scrutiny of media coverage. Studying his technique for deflecting criticism.

Trying to understand his position in the dispute with Terry Dean after he benched his senior quarterback halfway through the year, causing a firestorm of controversy.

And wrestling with the dilemma of a talented, but often unfocused wide receiver in Jack Jackson, the best player on the offensive unit.

Which is not to say there wasn't brilliance. Sometimes his play-calling was pure Phi Beta Kappa. His justice in dealing with disciplinary problems was swift and fair. And his ability to maintain such a high level of competition for the fifth straight season was downright astonishing.

The shape of the story changed somewhat as the season evolved.

In one single Saturday afternoon, Auburn devastated any dreams of national championships or Heisman trophies, but there was still the SEC championship to be won. An uncanny double-jeopardy fate would pit the Gators against their hated rival, Florida State, not once, but twice in a single season.

There were more story lines than a month of *Days Of Our Lives* and *All My Children* episodes rolled into one.

Although a labor of love, this book was also a day-to-day project that sometimes teetered on the brink of oblivion. My plan: Go as far as I can go until the money runs out, the obstacles get too big or the story dies. None of the above happened. The journey was an exhilarating one.

I enjoyed every minute. The renewal of old friendships and discovery of tiny unexpected pleasures and treasures kept me in high spirits, not the least of which was the chance to once again savor the pageantry of big-time Southern football.

I made new friends in the media in the five months of covering the Gators.

Several of us even started our own "Florida Cracker Boy" club, which was exclusive to natives of the state only. *Gainesville Sun* sports writers Mike Bianchi, Robbie Andreu and Pat Dooley and *Tampa Tribune* sports columnist Tom McEwen are the only members so far.

We have not yet voted on what privileges we Cracker Boys should be granted for our geographical blessing, but we think it entitles us to be snooty and grouse excessively about the Gators.

Actually, *Down Where The Old Gators Play* turned out to be a journal of many different journeys, not just the head coach and the author.

There were also the fascinating-but-tragic journeys of Terry Dean and Charley Pell, a player and a coach who have wound up in exile.

I was fortunate enough to be allowed in the inner circle of Terry Dean's family and I also befriended Charley Pell and his wife, Ward, neither of whom I had previously met.

As is the case of all journeys, the final destination of the Gator quarterback and the former head coach at Florida have yet to be permanently decided.

Pell began picking up the pieces of his life early in 1995. After a taste of coaching in the 1995 Hula Bowl and failing to land a college position, just before his 54th birthday he took a high school coaching/counselor position in Winter Haven.

Dean, hoping to be drafted in the first six rounds and play quarterback in the NFL, was not chosen by any team and began seeking a free agent contract, finally signing with the Canadian Football League.

There was also the journey home for the Gators' All-American, Jackson, who returned to Mississippi for a game against Ole Miss, the school he spurned for Florida because of the racial prejudice which he felt abounded on campus.

Jackson would become the focal point of a team disciplinary action, but rebounded for an All-American season, forgoing his senior year to come out early for the NFL draft. He was a fourth-round pick of the Chicago Bears.

What I will remember, most of all, from this journey: Returning to the press box on assignment, this time as a freelance writer for the *New York Times*, and trying to keep pace with the frenetic action of the 31-31 "Choke at Doak" tie between Florida and Florida State. . .Feasting on that Southern delicacy, boiled peanuts, with my sister, Shirley, at Seiler's Produce stand just north of Ocala on the way to a home game in Gainesville. . .Sitting along press row with my old friends--especially Frank Frangie and David Lamm of WNZS in Jacksonville and Jack Hairston of *Gator Pipeline*. . Football down South: Experiencing and understanding the intrinsic impact of football on life in places like Oxford, Mississipppi and Knoxville, Tennessee. . .The first "radio time out" I'd ever witnessed first-hand, this one for WSM in Nashville during the Florida-Vandy game (the Commodores rarely have their games on TV). . .Listening closely to the lyrics as the crowd sang *We Are The Boys From Old Florida* and restraining myself from chiming in on the part, *"down where the old Gators play"*. . .And, finally, enjoying that beautiful Saturday morning drive through the rolling greenbelt of Central Florida from Ocala to Gainesville. . .On the return trip at night to my home, listening to Southeastern Conference football announcers so cleverly embellish the air waves on the car radio. . .And, of course, the privilege of going back home to the very house where I grew up as a child.

One extra-added bonus that I did not anticipate came in May of 1995 when I attended a special Ocala High School reunion for all the classes of the 1950s and visited with many old friends.

It gave me a chance to reflect deeper, because many of their lives were so similar to mine--especially those who lived and died with the Gators then. And especially "The Four M's" who were together for the first time in more than 30 years: Yours truly, Ed Monarchik, Don Meyers and Bill Milby.

As for those classmates who went astray and wound up at Florida State (Charlotte Ponder and Judy Wallace, that's you!), don't despair. No book on Florida football could be complete without several chapters on the rivalry with FSU.

While I can honestly say nobody from our class grew up dreaming of playing in the garnet and gold colors, it is true that since we all graduated from high school in 1956, that's changed. Many kids today aspire to play for FSU and the Seminoles have built a football powerhouse to be envied.

This book, however, is about Gator football, so we went after the experts for key research. As an addendum, we polled an illustrious panel of leading sports media figures in Florida on the all-time greatest Gator players, teams and games, which you will find in the back of this book.

Finally, my feelings about returning to my childhood home were best expressed in a verse from the hand of Thomas Wolfe which my wife had framed and gave me as a homecoming gift:

And again, again, in this house
I feel beneath my tread,
The creak of the old stairs, the
whitewashed walls, the feel
of darkness and the house asleep.
And I think
'I was a child here.'

--Thomas Wolfe

I. the last guy out of the press box

Some of my finest years in newspapering were spent with my training wheels hitched to an old Royal portable typewriter, rationalizing the fickle fate of Florida football. I pounced on those keys many an autumn Saturday afternoon in Florida Field press box.

This was my first journalistic obsession, searching for the conspiratorial forces which prohibited the Gators from their rightful place in history. The days usually ended with darkness descending over the stadium as I pored over that old Royal, calling out the demons.

Along about every November there came a chilling wind which blew paper cups across the stadium's concrete floor, carrying the dirge of familiar broken dreams. Words came hard. Novembers were especially cold and cruel.

The eerie sound of those cups dancing in the wind, scraping across the concrete, was the grim reminder of another season almost consumed by winter hibernation, of promises left unfulfilled down on the grassy stage below.

It was there, incarcerated by press box solitude hours after the game had ended, that a young aspiring writer soon realized the limitations of his verbal repertoire and the struggle ensued.

'Words came hard. Novembers were especially cold and cruel.'

No matter how you write it, you can't transform a defeat into victory.

I never figured out if I was the last one to leave the press box because I was more conscientious than others, or just slower and not as skilled. Some days it was writer's purgatory. Other times it was inexplicable bliss. Either way, it was what I was born to do. Or so I thought.

Seemingly, I have always been emotionally tethered to Gator football and often professionally linked as well.
For the first 12 years of my writing career, the Gators were my primary beat.

Sometimes they consumed my entire sports psyche, because they were woven into the very fabric of our lives. And when I found out a newspaper would pay me to write about them and give me a free seat in the press box, I felt like Willie Sutton holding up a bank.

You want to know how important the Gators were to us? One of my former journalism classmates at Florida who grew up in Jacksonville and worked at the *Florida Times-Union* once claimed this huge aspiration for career advancement: To someday become worthy enough so he could be assigned to write the lead story on the Florida-Georgia game.

Hubert Mizell never realized his dream. Instead. he had to "settle" for becoming lead columnist of the *St. Petersburg Times.*

The telephone would be ringing any moment. As I awaited the return call of Florida football coach Steve Spurrier on this sticky Friday September morning in 1994, I stood in the living room of the six-room frame house where my parents brought me home from the hospital as an infant.

Feeling, paradoxically, both old and young, I reflected on the seeds of my passion for Gator football planted here with the acorns and giant oak trees in Ocala, Florida.

For nearly the first 40 years of their affiliation with the Southeastern Conference, the Gators were a one-way ticket to Heartbreak Hotel. For the first 57 SEC seasons, they never won a title of any kind which they could keep, except Most Overrated Team. Yet somehow love and adoration transcended all that woe.

Along with the Vanderbilt Commodores, the Gators shared the embarrassing distinction of never having won an official SEC title in football until Spurrier came along as coach.

(Charley Pell and Galen Hall's' team won the SEC in 1984, but the SEC presidents made Florida give it back because of NCAA violations.)

Still, in Central Florida, the Gators always aroused pathos hotter than the July Florida sun and were favored with a spirit of charitable forgiveness that inspired a fresh wave of eternal optimism every fall. Our faith was indomitable, if not always warranted.

Some saw it as dreams of ignorance.

"A long time before they won anything," said my friend Dan Jenkins, noted novelist, golf columnist and college football junkie, "Gator fans had the arrogance of Alabama and the tradition of Wake Forest."

The predictable "wait 'til next year" lament was part of the spring ritual in Central Florida that often served as the official closure on last autumn's disappointments.

That now infamous Gator phrase had originated from a prayer for Gator football published by the student newspaper in 1912. *The Florida Alligator* plagiarized it. That slogan came from the battle cry of an arch rival, Stetson, the Baptist college in nearby DeLand.

As the '94 season approached, Gator faithful were praying they wouldn't be hearing that sad refrain again.

Even in a season fraught with so much promise, however, there would sometimes be a re-emergence of the dark side of Florida football which hovered overhead like a cloud of quiet despair.

As a writer and still-practicing journalist, I was intrigued by what might lie ahead for Spurrier and his prodigious team in his fifth season as head coach.

Why, I wondered, do we so readily form eternal allegiances of our college youth which bind us for life? After all these years, why do I still care?

And now that the 1994 Gators were the No. 1 ranked college football team in the country, wasn't I guilty of bandwagon jumping, something that I always deplored in fans?

On many occasions since I've left sports writing, newspapers and the Gator beat, I've reflected back on those days as a young sports columnist who wrote so passionately about the seemingly infinitesimal, yet catastrophic difference between victory and defeat.

Sometimes those days seem so adolescent and even though they remain some of the happiest times of my life, I truly never had a desire to re-live them or yearn to go back.

Then I experienced a cosmic flashback that day in April of 1994 on a visit to Gainesville, Florida, where I had gone to speak to the Gainesville Quarterback Club. This was about to turn into a pilgrimage for me.

By this point I have virtually reached the journalistic-objectivity-be-damned stage of life about most things, no longer handcuffed by the constraints of a sports writer's "proper conduct," unless I am on assignment to write for a newspaper or magazine.

If I want to root for a team or a player, I do so in the privacy of my living room without feeling remorseful.

Or maybe I might even swear at an official or a coach and throw a pillow at the TV.

Long after the typewriter was put to rest and newspapering went away, I remained intrigued by the Gators, though always striving not to let my personal prejudice reflect in my work.

On this night, as the guest speaker before more than 300 Gainesville Quarterback club members, I felt the need to declare my allegiances as a Florida man.

As Spurrier warmly welcomed me back to the friendly confines of the Florida campus, I felt a sense of belonging--maybe even obligation.

So I decided to tailor my speech to that of a fan instead of a journalist.

It worked, because subsequently my well-intentioned sincerity bridged a gap with the audience and I experienced a rare bonding in which sports writers seldom indulge, because it is a bit risky.

For me, no longer a full-time newspaper man, it was a risk worth taking because I was hoping that I could allow myself to feel the true passion of college football again at the grass roots level.

Florida's basketball team had just won the school's first berth in the Final Four. The football team, coming off a triumph in the Sugar Bowl over West Virginia, was hoisting its third SEC championship pennant in four years. In all, a good time to be a Gator fan, especially after all the shame heaped on the school by NCAA sanctions during the '80s.

Earlier that day at spring practice, I could sense that Spurrier was enthusiastic about the team he would coach in the fall of '94. He had invited me out to stand next to him on the field so that I could witness, first hand, this potential juggernaut as his players ran through a controlled, half-speed workout.

Though excited about this team, Spurrier seemed uneasy about his immediate future--without any justification that I could see.

He talked that day about coaches' popularity declining. Jimmy Johnson had just resigned from the Cowboys.

"Sometimes people get tired of coaches," he said.

"Johnson stayed five years at Oklahoma State, five years at Miami and now five years at the Cowboys. People may be getting tired of me."

I couldn't see how Johnson's resignation pertained to him and wondered if he wasn't just feeling the sting of media criticism.

At the time, Spurrier was being chastised by some writers about his decision to demote popular defensive coordinator Ron Zook to special teams coach.

It was almost a personal affront to Spurrier to be second-guessed for making a coaching change on his staff. Though I didn't realize it at the time, that was the first clue about the enormous pressure that he must face on almost a daily basis.

It was also an example of what his critics say is Spurrier's great disdain toward those who dare to challenge him or his methods. They say he treats it as treason.

Already considered the best coach in Florida history, it was difficult to imagine anything but good times ahead for this former Heisman Trophy winner.

That matter would be resolved soon. Spurrier's long-term security would be assured a few months later in the summer with the signing of a new contract that would earn him in excess of $700,000 per year through the turn of the century.

In a difficult year, when the strain of a high stakes game began to show, there were times that those who of us followed him closely throughout the season feared Spurrier might crack, or be enticed by NFL teams, or even become so irritated by the media or so provoked by the mis-conduct of his players that he might go AWOL.

After all, it suddenly became fashionable for coaches to make sudden and emotional exits.

As I worked on this book during the winter of '94-'95, a shocking revelation occurred about a friend mine who was a subject of my second book in 1985.

Dan Issel resigned as head coach of the Denver Nuggets, saying that his heart wasn't in it, that he would never coach again and that "I didn't like what I had become."

Although Issel never really gave a detailed explanation behind his decision, clearly part of it was a mid-life course correction. It was curious timing, since the Nuggets had just announced plans for a new state-of-the-art, $132 million downtown arena.

The resignation was an effort to resolve the conflict within Issel's soul, because he didn't like the direction coaching was taking him. He was tired of athletes who wouldn't give 100 per cent effort, something that was inbred in him as a player.

As a Hall of Famer, Issel had rarely been criticized. As a coach, he was often caught in the cross-hairs of what he considered unfair criticism. I could see similarities between Issel's plight and that of Spurrier's, whom I had just followed for a 13-game season.

A few weeks prior to Issel's departure, the best coach in University of Colorado football history, Bill McCartney, quit for personal reasons. McCartney, a spiritual person, said he intended to devote more time to his family, especially his wife Lindy.

McCartney never really gave any other reason for resigning from one of the best college football programs in America--a program he had resurrected from the ashes just over a decade ago. Why quit now?

After his last team beat Notre Dame in the Fiesta Bowl and wound up with a top five ranking, McCartney bade goodbye, leaving the following words on his message machine: "The McCartneys have gone fishin'."

Why are people willing to give up these high-profile, high-paying jobs, regardless of consequences, especially after they go through so much to get them?

There are common threads that bind them.

■They were among the best at what they did;

■They were either in, or just around the corner from their peak years;

■They had built programs from the ground up;

■They left only after achieving considerable success, in search of new horizons or different lifestyles.

■None did it for the money.

A little more than 24 hours before the kickoff of the No. 1 ranked Florida Gators' 1994 season, the air was pregnant with expectation. All Gator fans knew they were on the precipice of elusive greatness in this first step against New Mexico State the next night, feeble though the Aggies may be.

Tomorrow night was the start of the large new dream at Florida Field in Gainesville, a place I had been hundreds of times before, but never when it felt so much like I was going to a jubilee and a family reunion.

It wasn't so much the caliber of opposition that counted. This was an official ribbon-cutting of The Dream Season that had been forever coming and was only a mirage in times past.

I walked up the street to the neighborhood Kwik King. When I returned, there was a message on my machine, laced with Spurrier's unmistakable touch of East Tennessee twang:

"What's happening my man?. . .I'll see you tomorrow night. It should be an exciting night. Number one! Your old school is number one in the country and you've lived to see it! That's something right there!"

Steve Spurrier was right, I had lived to see it, and that ***was*** something right there. So I set out for Gainesville to watch the last practice before the Saturday night opener.

It was the first of many trips during the fall that I would make from my outpost in Ocala, where Gator fever is more contagious than measles. And sometimes as painful.

Ocala, Florida, Marion County, Kingdom of the Sun, Home of Kentucky Derby winners Needles and Carry Back, can be prison to some, paradise to others. I tried to make to that point back in 1981, as emcee at our 25th reunion of the 1956 Ocala High School senior class in an essay I prepared:

"Ocala might have been the perfect town in which to grow up, and at the perfect time. We were too old for Vietnam and too young for Korea. Our parents has taught us the lessons of the Depression, but we never had to endure their hardships. Our lives were unencumbered by the computer age of the eighties, the political scandal of the seventies and the social strife of the sixties.

"Drugs were something you bought at the prescription counter of Bittings or Bennett's drug stores, which is where we also bought ice cream sodas and sundaes. Getting stoned meant somebody threw rocks at you. Cars were easily recognized because they had simple names: Fords, Chevys, Pontiacs, Oldsmobiles, Buicks, etc.--not Pintos or Camaros or Fairlanes or Regals or such. We were the Silent Generation--silent, because we never learned about protest and rebellion until James Dean came along in *Rebel Without A Cause.*

"Then we became Rebels without causes until Elvis taught us about Rock 'N Roll. Ocala in the mid-fifties. . .The Ike Years. . .A 'joint' was somewhere you went to go jukin', not something you smoked. . .We wore pony tails (girls) and duck tails (boys). . .White bucks and ballerinas. . .Letter sweaters and crinolines. . .We (boys) put Hollywood glass pack mufflers on our cars and drove them to Woodfields, Silvers Springs and the Lime Pit, where we turned our radios to WLAC in Nashville (rhythm and blues) or WCKY in Cincinnati (country) or perhaps even WWL in New Orleans (jazz) or WBT in Charlotte (pop). First, of course, we took our dates to a movie and then for a cherry Coke at The Big D or Chicken Ranch.

"We had no zip codes or area codes or credit cards or even bank account numbers back then. Life was like a G-rated movie, but, of course, we didn't have X-rated movies then. We had Debbie Reynolds as Tammy, Yul Brenner as The King and Ingrid Bergman, who was trying to prove she was Anastasia. That year the Andrea Doria collided with the Stockholm off Nantucket. . .They made the first Trans-Atlantic telephone call. . .And Nixon was only *vice* president.

"For a dollar you could buy over three gallons of gas, which could easily get you down to Johnson's Beach and back on a summer night, where you'd jitterbug your cares away or, maybe later, go out in the cars and have orange fights. A dollar, in fact, would get you and your date into the Marion Theater and a root beer apiece at the Chicken Ranch, which was cheaper than the Big D.

"It was a simple life, a good life, one many of us have wished our children could have had. But, of course, it cannot be. Some of us who wanted to stay had to leave Ocala and some who wanted to leave had to stay behind--and many of us will always wonder which was right. We came from a perfect town in a perfect time."

Ocala was never "prison" to me, perhaps because I was one who left. In the spring of '93, I came back to sample a little bit of "paradise." For the first time in more than 20 years, I slept in the bedroom of my childhood home.

After the death of my step-father, Bernard Cannon, The Martin Place property reverted back to my sister and me. Gifted with a house full of furniture from my mother-in-law, Lori Byrd, and granted the approval of my sister, Shirley Lovell, to move in, I took up residence in my hometown.

Though the neighborhood has changed, it felt very much like it did in my youth, where most of my sports adventures emanated from a beautiful console Zenith radio.

The Dairy Queen on the corner of Silver Springs Boulevard has long since been gone. You can't hear the wind singing anymore through the Australian pine trees that my father planted the year I was born. They've been uprooted and replaced by dogwoods and redbuds.

The gas station on the north side has been leveled. The poinsettias and roses that grew at the hand of my mother, Margaret O'Quinn Martin Cannon, don't bloom anymore. The mulberry tree in front is gone. But mother's Camellia bush still reigns supreme. My sister and I also planted a orange and grapefruit tree on the south side of the house and it is my dream one day to harvest my breakfast from them, so I keep a close watch.

Ozzie and Harriet could have raised the Nelson family there and Norman Rockwell could have painted our "East Street," which is what it was called then, before the goofy quadrant system was adopted.

The Thompsons, Buddy and Rose and their three kids, Rosebud, John and Billy, are gone from the house next door, but my nephew, Scott Lovell, and his new wife, Dawn, have moved in. The Simmons across the street have died and a chiropractor's office has taken root.

On the corner site of the old Work house is a shoe store. In the next block to the south, on a southeast corner, a second generation member of the Williams, family, Pat, still runs his tax business there.

Next door to the Williams residence is the sturdy brick home of our good family friends, the Cullisons, which now belongs to oldest son, Jerry, brother of my friend, Jackie, and his sisters, Elsie, and the late Bessie, one of our best athletes.

For the most part, "East Street" has survived urban blight. That only underscores what I've always believed: The best way to keep a neighborhood up is for the people who care about it to move back in it.

It was a wonderful experience, sleeping in my old bedroom after more than two decades of being gone, like walking into a virtual reality episode of *The Twilight Zone.*

On that beautiful spring night, my wife and I lay there, windows open, soaking up the magnificent smells and sounds of the night. The Mockingbird in the 150-year-old oak tree out back serenaded us with oldies. I swear he's been there 50 years and he never sounded better. The same bird all these years perhaps?

It felt like, smelled like, sounded like home. Especially after hearing the freight train rumble through downtown Ocala around midnight.

"I can remember hearing that same train many nights as a young boy," I told Joni. "I always wondered where it was going. And if it would be taking me to some place exciting one day."

That train whistle is not nearly so lonesome now. It is a comforting sound, a gentle reminder of all the places I have been and seen in 30 years. Once that whistle beckoned me to places in my dreams, but was now calling me back to my childhood home, where I had waited for what seemed like an eternity on the promises of the Florida Gators to take wing. And now the vigil was on once again.

II. where have you gone Chuck Hunsinger?

Back in the days when the rivers and streams of Florida still ran clear and wild turkey and deer roamed the Ocala National Forest in abundance, Charlie, or "Chuck," Hunsinger first galloped through my life and forever changed my sense of priorities.

Despite never meeting Chuck or actually ever seeing him play, he was destined to become my first real sports hero, if for no other reason than the fascination with his name.

Emmit Smith he was not. But he ***was*** a University of Florida Gator football player, the first I ever knew about. And nothing in sports was as politically or culturally correct for a young Florida boy approaching puberty about the time Harry Truman was starting his second term in the White House.

For a boy in a small town, heroes were hard to come by, because all the big superstars lived in far away places. Joe DiMaggio may have been The King of Yankee Stadium, Stan Musial The Man at Sportsman's Park in St. Louis and Ted Williams The Splendid Splinter of Fenway Park.

But for me, Chuck Hunsinger cast the biggest shadow along the banks of the St. Johns River, south to the Everglades and north along the Gulf of Mexico to the panhandle.

'. . .college football was king. And the Florida Gators were royal family.'

Even though I didn't know how good Hunsinger really was--in fact, I barely new *of* him--I staked my claim on his reputation.

In the Deep South, which Central Florida was even more akin to back in the fifties and sixties, college football was king. And the Florida Gators were royal family. Even though the Gators played one town north of Ocala, 37 miles up the road, they also belonged to our city, too.

We always liked to point out with pride that University of Florida started in Ocala as East Florida Seminary back in 1852, even if that was long before the 1906 birth of football.

Ocala was a semi-rural, semi-agrarian town with a cowboy influence emerging during the Fat Stock Show week. Adult men were permitted to act like children. Anyone seen walking around the court house during Fat Stock Show without a beard or western attire was unceremoniously dunked in water troughs.

We took our cowboy stuff seriously. We also took our Gators seriously.

There wasn't much competition to rival Florida football. Florida State had just gone coed, changing its name from Florida State College of Women. Besides, Tallahassee was a four-hour car ride away. Miami, was, well, of course Miami, which was 350 miles down the peninsular, somewhere around Cuba.

Like most Florida natives, I grew up loving the Gators. The proliferation of pro franchises in the state was still eons away. There were no Dolphins, no Jaguars, no Bucs, no Lightning, no Magic, no Marlins, no Heat and, perhaps thankfully, no Devil Rays. Even if there had been, it wouldn't have mattered.

There was only the Gators, but they made us rich in spirit and purpose.

The World Series always finished a poor second in our neighborhood to the Florida-Georgia football game.

Even the Series couldn't replace that classic border state battle in Jacksonville's Gator Bowl. Florida vs. Georgia was once dubbed "the world's largest outdoor cocktail party," a euphemism for a big drunk.

To me, "Take Me Out To The Ball Game" was a song about going to Florida Field on a Saturday until I finally made it to Yankee Stadium and heard it played there. Cultural bias, I guess.

Boys living in Central Florida back then were reaching out for real heroes that we could touch in our own backyard. So I adopted Chuck, although I knew very little about him.

We needed Chuck, or someone like him, and we needed the Gators to validate our existence, to give our lives meaning. So the quality of our existence ebbed and flowed with Gator wins and losses.

We didn't have college games on TV. There were no ESPN Sports Center highlights or Gator clips on local TV. I couldn't afford a ticket to the game. So Chuck played in the only place he could for me: On my father's Zenith radio with the big green eye. Or in the black and white of newspaper photos. And the theater of my mind, which still contains the most powerful images of my youth.

Without real images, you went for names. The first name which enamored me was "Choo Choo"--Choo Choo Justice, the All-American running back. But he played for North Carolina and it would have been considered treason to adopt a "foreign" hero.

Hunsinger was, in fact, merely a pretty fair country running back for the lowly Gators, albeit of All-Southeastern Conference stature.

But exaggeration is the hallmark of the Southern culture. So aggrandizement of your Saturday hero and embellishment of the mediocre was an accepted practice.

You were even permitted to embrace mythological terms. Hunsinger became the Godzilla of sports, bigger than life, the greatest football player in the universe to me. And to most people in North Central Florida, the Gators ***were*** life.

Today, the recollections come harder and it's difficult to distinguish historical fact from boyhood fiction. But with the help of books like *The Gators,* written by *Tampa Tribune* sports columnist Tom McEwen (1974, The Strode Publishers) and *Golden Era II* (1994, Hillsboro Printing and Lithographing) by Julian Clarkson, slowly the memories begin to come back.

Not until reading Clarkson's book did I know that Hunsinger hailed from Harrisburg, Illinois, or that he had actually played service football at Jacksonville Naval Air Station against such superstars as Choo Choo and Georgia great Charlie Trippi.

I do remember that Hunsinger had a song written about him, *Hunsinger The Humdinger.* The book *The Gators* confirmed that fact, complete with sheet music, so this was not a total figment of my childhood imagination.

I never learned to sing it--never wanted to--but did recall that even from an early age I realized the lyrics were awful.

I hadn't known that *Hunsinger The Humdinger* was actually written by a sports writer, Zipp Newman of the Birmingham News, in 1947. After reading them, you can see why the song never made it:

"Hunsinger's a humdinger
Not ever will he linger
In ramming a ball
Thru the enemy's wall

"No player is torrider
Than this lad from Florida
Hun-singer the Hum-dinger
You ought to see him go."

Looking back on it now, Hunsinger deserved better.

Though a symbol of pride and respect, Chuck Hunsinger was just the Gator Du Jour. A few years later, we had Rick Casares, the first big football and basketball star at Florida to attract national attention. Then Charlie LaPradd, then Jackie Simpson, then Jimmy Dunn, then Steve Spurrier, then Richard Trapp, then Larry Smith, then Carlos Alvarez and John Reaves, then Nat Moore, then Wes Chandler, then Neal Anderson, then Kerwin Bell, then Emmitt Smith. . .

Plus many more I have not named in between and since then. Those were just some of my personal favorites and it no way reflects which players may have been superior. And unlike Hunsinger, I did see all of *them* play.

We always cling to the memories of our first hero and in our case we had so little else to cheer about. Gator football by 1950 had produced no championships, one All-American and nothing close to national recognition.

"The first Gator player anybody ever heard of," said Jenkins, himself a long-suffering TCU alumnus and fan, "was Casares."

I couldn't convince him, even now, about the legendary status of Chuck Hunsinger.

It's true that for the beginning in 1906 and pretty much up through the Eisenhower years, Florida had perfected the art of mediocrity and was a lukewarm, second-rate program except for the 1928 team.

I had heard a little and read some about the famous '28 bunch coached by Charles Bachman, who produced a near-perfect 8-1 record and then suffered a heart-breaking 13-12 loss at the hands of Gen. Bob Neyland's Tennessee team.

Otherwise, up through the years to 1960, there had been some lean decades. There wasn't a wealth of talent between Dale Van Sickel--a member of Bachman's '28 Gators and Florida's first All-American--and Chuck Hunsinger.

No wonder, then, we were always looking for a Moses in orange and blue. And until Spurrier emerged in the mid-sixties, winning the Heisman Trophy his senior year, it appeared we were doomed for a lifetime of wannabes and whatmightabeens.

That green eye of that huge Zenith console radio in a walnut cabinet dominated the corner of the dining room like a Cyclops when I was a boy. Many times my father had knelt before that radio in reverence, listening to the World War II news reports.

I took comfort in knowing that my dad, Wilton Martin Sr., was dutifully watching for the family and, should the Japanese or Germans invade our Florida shores, surely he would be first in the neighborhood to know.

The world of radio was a magic carpet ride back in the late forties and early fifties, taking you places that you never dreamed possible. It just never occurred to me that you could actually hear broadcasts of sporting events over it.

If I shimmied up one of the Australian pines outside and affixed a wire to a limb, I could even pull that voice of Harry Caray out of the skies as he broadcast Cardinal baseball games from a far away place in St. Louis called KMOX, just like my older friend Tommy Herren had promised.

It was also the influence of Tommy that first piqued my interest in the Gators. Tommy was a halfback on the Ocala Junior High team in my sister Shirley's class. When I was in sixth grade, I would ride my bike over to watch his junior high team's practice and cheer for Tommy Herren.

Tom Sr., his dad, would often talk to Tommy Jr. about sports, something my dad never did.

Sometimes I would walk home from practice and listen to Tommy talk sports with his high school friend, Jimmy Stellogeannis, who was a star athlete for the Ocala Wildcats and one day would become my friend, too. They talked a lot about the Florida Gators. If Tommy Herren and Jimmy Stellogeannis cheered for the Gators, I knew they had to be good. I longed for the day I could talk with them about such an important subject.

That Zenith radio became my direct line to Otis Boggs, Voice of the Gators.

It was in this house where I was standing, more than 45 years ago, that I had first heard Otis describing the feats of these wonderful, yet virtually invisible Gators--invisible to the naked eye, but not the imagination of a young boy and his radio.

Otis is a kind and gentle soul who prided himself on showing restraint from total, unadulterated homerism. He didn't whine and cry like some of the other announcers when their teams weren't doing well.

But he did bastardize the English language to describe the spin of a football when it was punted.

I had picked up pronunciation of the word as "sparrel" from Boggs, a southern gentleman born in South Carolina.

Years later, although I had been told that the word "spiral" was not pronounced like "barrel," I had a hard time believing it, because that's how the Voice of the Gators had said it.

At about age 10, I would go to the closet for a green, hand-me-down wool sweater right about kickoff time and stuff wash clothes under the shoulders to simulate a football uniform.

Once properly uniformed, I would run through the living and dining rooms, stiff-arming the would-be tackles of chairs, sofas and tables.

Something about these Gators kept me transfixed on them from an early age.

Imagine my excitement the day I was asked to attend my first game. My eighth-grade classmate, the late Alexander Moseley (Zandy) Collins and his parents, Martha and Alec, drove me to Gainesville and bought my ticket, an act of kindness for which I will be eternally grateful.

From the first Saturday on I was hooked and my intuition was running rampant, in a foot race with my imagination. Somehow I knew that my destiny one day would be intertwined in the Gators--in my fantasies as an All-American quarterback, perhaps.

And when I dreamt about my future it was always in an orange and blue uniform, even when I was wearing a green wool sweater. Through high school, my buddies Ed Monarchik and Don Meyers and I would latch on to the Gators' fantasy and ride those dreams hard..

Monarchik chose Florida Southern as his college, but Meyers and I went on to become Florida students. The closest I would ever get to wearing the colors orange and blue was in a Gator baseball uniform, pitching for the freshman team and playing a partial sophomore season for coach Dave Fuller.

Having failed at that, I decided to write about it, so I joined the staff of the *Florida Alligator* and began the journey down the road of ink-stained wretches.

I would come to learn that with the wearing of the school colors came a certain amount of baggage, not the least of which is Gator paranoia.

If there is a curse that goes with the possession of the Hope Diamond, then there must be a hex on for the Florida Gators when greatness is expected of their football team. Pain and suffering are prerequisites for Gator fans. But Steve Spurrier is helping ease some of that pain.

III. it's off to see The Swamp Fox

It didn't take long for that Gator paranoia to set in. There was a certain frailty about the lofty No. 1 status. So in the late summer of 1994 one of my first trips from Colorado back to Florida, I made a note on my tape recorder that while this elitist stuff was new and exciting to Gator fans, "we all have to wonder how long it will last."

Just two nights before the No. 1 ranked Gators were due to kick off their '94 season, another highly ranked team brushed up against disaster.

Arizona, which Sports Illustrated had dubbed as its No. 1 college football team for the '94 pre-season, narrowly escaped upset at the hands of a weak Georgia Tech team.

New Mexico State was a 44-point underdog to the Gators, but there was still a certain amount of skepticism. And this foray into the national limelight still didn't feel comfortable because many fans didn't feel they belonged among the privileged elite.

Was this team overrated? Again? The fragile nature of the ranking was a little disconcerting.

Although not the first time the Gators had been ranked No. 1, it was the first time they'd played at home as the nation's top-ranked team.

'You never truly forget the college football team of your heart.'

A few years prior they had made a cameo appearance on the top rung. Back in 1985, Galen Hall's team enjoyed the celebrity of No. 1 for one week before getting stung by Georgia in Jacksonville, 24-3.

As the 1994 Gators were unveiling their newfound stature in a place known as "The Swamp," all of us, including coach Spurrier, were curious about the sound of the cheer "We're No. 1!" when it was really an accurate proclamation for a change.

Nothing in sports seems to arouse the loyalty and passion of fans as does the success of your alma mater.

You might change houses or jobs or even spouses. Maybe you might even change your loyalties to a professional team when you change towns. Like your first sweetheart, you never truly forget the college football team of your heart.

That thought crossed my mind as, at age 56, I walked up the stairs to the coaches' office at the University of Florida to meet with Spurrier. I hoped he would grant me a few minutes of pre-season, pre-game briefing.

It was a friendly welcome, but later I would learn this was to be the last meeting of its kind until after the season ended. Spurrier wears his blinders and his official game face 24 hours a day, seven days a week. Private meetings with journalists--even old friends--are an indulgence Spurrier rarely would allow himself this season.

That aside, he welcomed me and we both reveled a bit together in the national attention for our old school.

"The funny part about it is that I've never really been associated with a team that was No. 1 in anything," Spurrier said as he took me on a quick tour of the old photos and some of the other lesser memorabilia in his office. "Except one time in high school (Science High, Johnson City, Tennessee) our baseball team won the state championship."

It is hard for me not to like Steve Spurrier, although he can be a lightning rod, outspoken and controversial.

I have always been a fan of his, as well as a friend, long before he was winning football games at Florida. Though he has detractors among his peers, in the media and among fans, nobody denies he produces results. And he is honest to a fault, something that keeps him constantly embroiled in controversy.

Many of his critics say he is self-absorbed; that he has little loyalty to his players, assistant coaches or friends; that he often reacts out of arrogance or disdain; and that he would sell his grandmother down the river for a win.

Having never been up close to him during a season when he was coaching, I didn't know quite what to expect, but I found that perception of him difficult to fathom.

I would also discover that very few people really know Steve Spurrier, even those who think they do--including me.

As I observed Spurrier in this different role, on the hot-seat, I would come to learn why others might feel those criticisms were justified, even if I didn't agree with them.

Our relationship had gone back to the days when he was an All-American quarterback and Heisman Trophy winner and I was a young writer for the *Ocala Star-Banner* and *Today* newspaper in Cocoa, Florida. I covered him both as a college and pro player and occasionally we played a round of golf together.

We weren't intimate friends, but we kept in touch. When he went to play for the San Francisco 49ers and I ghost-wrote a column for six state papers under Spurrier's name, entitled *"Passing Thoughts."*

Many years and quite a few coaching jobs and newspaper sports columns had come and gone between then and now. A lot of thoughts have been passed on. And Spurrier has since risen to the top of his profession as one of the two or three brightest coaches in football, college or pro.

He fulfilled a lifetime dream by making the ultimate journey back home to Gainesville, where he had spent the major part of his adult life. And now he was preparing to embark on a season that held the greatest potential of any he had ever known as a coach.

On the Friday before the start of his fifth season at Florida, he appeared fresh, relaxed and equal to the task. Looking around his office, one might have surmised that Spurrier was golf coach instead of football coach: Three putters lined up against one wall. . .a round container with more than 15 drivers. . .Photos of himself and Jack Nicklaus and Dolly Parton and other celebrities at golf pro-ams.

Spurrier is an avid golfer, a single digit handicap, but he puts his clubs away for the football season as August practice draws nigh.

As a golfer, Spurrier has been known to thrive on pressure. I recall how that was proven out once when we were playing together in a Gator Bowl Tournament on Amelia Island in northeast Florida back in 1990.

Steve announced that if he could hit his 9-iron close to the pin on the last hole and make the putt, our team would stand a good chance of winning the tournament.

I wondered how he knew that we were even in contention, since there were no scoreboards.

Indeed, he knocked the short iron to within six feet, made the putt for birdie and our team won. I still use the Ping putter that I got for a prize. Spurrier has always had an amazing sense of where he stands in relationship to his competition.

And how did his '94 Gator stack up with the opposition? It was going to be a test to see how he might handle the pressure of coaching the nation's No. 1 team--how it may change his strategy or approach to the game. He insisted he wasn't planning to treat his players any different.

This was a young team, probably a bit overrated in Spurrier's mind--if you could read it. And he was trying to convince himself that this wasn't going to be Armageddon if they weren't ranked No. 1 at the end of the season.

Although off the record he predicted that they probably wouldn't win it all, we both knew that the zeal for a national championship was burning deep in his heart .

Yet on this day, he didn't appear the least bit uptight. He was desperately trying not to convey any extra pressure to his younger players.

"If one of these freshmen running backs (Elijah Williams or Fred Taylor) drops a pass or two or fumbles the ball, that's just going to be life--they're still going to play," said Spurrier.

"We're going to try to 'coach them up' not to be to tight, so they will believe 'if I fumble, coach is still going to play me in the game.' Now if he fumbles four or five times, he might be in trouble!"

Trying to make some sense out of how his team had arrived at this juncture, he said: "I don't even know how good a team we are right now. We're No. 1 because we beat West Virginia, 41-7, (in the 1994 Sugar Bowl). The voters said, 'those guys must be pretty good.' Everything went right that night. Who knows where we are? It just means we're judged right now to be No. 1.

“I said all summer if we're pre-season No. 1 that would be wonderful, because I'd like to be No. 1 for one week in my life rather than never, ever! It's not that big a deal if we're not No. 1 next week. There's no guarantee. If we don't play very well and FSU or Nebraska or somebody wins big-time, they may go to No. 1."

With almost the same precision Spurrier had predicted his successful 9-iron shot and tournament-winning birdie, he was unknowingly forecasting the future.

The books on Spurrier's office shelf might surprise you. Although not a voracious reader, he gleans bits and pieces from various authors with different philosophies.

For instance, after a tough loss at Syracuse in 1991, Spurrier picked up a copy of "Bo" by legendary ex-coach Michigan Bo Schembechler. If Spurrier's offense is liberal Democrat, then Bo's was to the right of Rush Limbaugh.

Yet it was the persistence of Schembechler's philosophy that "running teams are tougher than passing teams" which led Spurrier to alter his offensive game plan the next week against Mississippi State in 1991. Florida went on to a 10-2 season and Sugar Bowl berth. Later he saw Schembechler on an airplane, told him of his influence and "he got a big kick out of it I think."

He also read books by New York Knicks coach Pat Riley ("The Winner Within") because his teams "play hard and play smart"--one of his favorite resources. . .A biography of former Alabama coach Paul "Bear" Bryant. . .A biography on Raiders quarterback Jeff Hostetler ("somebody gave it to me") and several others. But none had significant enough impact to persuade him to change his philosophy, except Riley, who he remembered had said, "once in a while you've got to take a stand."

"You don't copy anybody else," Spurrier declared. "You've got to have your own style."

Indeed, Spurrier has copied nobody, either in his style of X's and O's or in his visor-slinging sideline decorum. Or, for that matter, his outspoken nature, although there would be a point during the season that he would take Riley's advice about "taking a stand."

He has built his own identity--an identity like none other in college football. It works for him, for his team and the place it plays, which he has nicknamed "The Swamp" for obvious reasons. But is also has its price.

Things around "The Swamp" smelled pretty good on this early September day. Time was, not so long ago, before Spurrier arrived in Gainesville (1990) that it stunk pretty badly. Florida was in trouble again with the NCAA and the athletic department was being depicted as something akin to a haven for John Dilllinger, Jesse James and Charles Manson.

Before Spurrier's arrival, there had been serious back-room discussion about the potential of a possible death penalty for various recruiting irregularities and alleged illegal payments in the basketball and football programs. Suddenly the entire sports program at the school was in danger of being put on a life support system, a fact that hardly went unnoticed by alumni at Florida State and Miami. At those two schools they were busy playing for national championships.

"I don't think things were all that bad," Spurrier said of the 1990 campaign. "When it was over and all was said and done, all the NCAA really had (on Galen Hall) was that he allegedly gave a player (Jarvis Williams) money in an envelope for child support to keep him from going to jail.

"They never proved that there was money in it. And to tell you the truth, I don't think there was."

Whether it was or not, Gator bashing was in vogue in the late eighties. So it was under that cloud that Spurrier had been hired from Duke. Shortly after his arrival in Gainesville there was a dramatic reversal in momentum for the bashers. And by the early nineties, the new favorite targets of derision were located in Tallahassee and Coral Gables instead.

Charges of payoffs to Seminole and Hurricane players by alumni were printed by national publications and were still under investigation at the writing of this book.

Several members of Bobby Bowden's national championship FSU team allegedly were treated to $6,000 shopping sprees at Foot Locker. One player was found guilty of perjury for lying about his role in the matter.

Others were paid, according to Sports Illustrated, for mythical jobs they never worked.

Hurricane players reportedly received payoffs from a "slush fund" created by former Miami players, given bonuses for exceptional performances on the field. And there was a major investigation pending on Miami's mis-use of funds involving Pell Grant money.

Florida loyalists hit by the slings and arrows aimed at the integrity of their program, from the quills of Seminole and Hurricane fans, began to feel vindicated.

They looked upon this news as mere justice, because the NCAA investigators were off their doorsteps and had taken up residence elsewhere in the state.

Somehow this was all written in the wind, however, as part of Steve Spurrier's fate.

Without the purge of 1989 which nailed head football coach Galen Hall and head basketball coach Norm Sloan for indiscretions, Spurrier likely wouldn't have gotten hired or been able to retrieve the Florida program from the ashes and put the Gators on the football map again. The NCAA giveth and the NCAA taketh away. Blessed be the NCAA.

For those long-suffering Gator fans who watched Spurrier, the player, elevate the Gators to a new standard of competition, it was an especially meaningful day when he signed on to coach his alma mater. And it was even more meaningful, after all those decades of mediocrity, to see just how high Spurrier could take them on this trip to the stars.

IV. only a slight case of Seminole bashing

Happy Days had arrived in Gainesville by the spring of 1994. After five years of penance for NCAA indiscretions, the Gators were returning to respectability under Spurrier, who brought a fresh new sense of pride and dignity to the job. He was also rapidly becoming the SEC's newest villain.

It didn't take long for the heat of the state rivalries to boil over. Despite early promises that he would put Miami back on the schedule--Spurrier attempted to do that before the SEC split into divisions--the Hurricanes and Gators were not going to play, an issue that would become a hotly contested one for South Florida journalists.

Meanwhile, there was a slight case of Seminole bashing by Spurrier in June of 1994. At least that's how it sounded to some, including Florida president John Lombardi.

At several boosters club or Gator Club meetings, Spurrier suggested FSU was an acronym for "Free Shoes University." Then he wondered aloud to a sports writer if the reason FSU had signed so many players in the state--the Seminoles have kicked butt in recruiting since the mid-eighties--might not be because of the solicitation of players with illicit goods.

'The shoes may have been free, but we paid dearly for everything else.'
--Bobby Bowden

It is common practice of coaches to poke fun at the opposition, especially when entertaining your own public. But Spurrier didn't stop there. He just couldn't resist another jibe at the Seminoles during one of the Gator Club meetings: "I hear there's a Gator in Tallahassee that's hated even more than I am," he said glibly. "An 'Investi-Gator.'"

Yet, Spurrier expresses respect for FSU.

Interestingly enough, during his press conference on the day he was hired, Dec. 31, 1989, Spurrier called FSU coach Bobby Bowden "probably the best coach in college football today."

While Spurrier was not directly implicating Bowden with his remarks about "Free Shoes," he was certainly casting aspersions on Bowden's program.

Bowden, trying to keep a sense of humor about it, chortled: "The shoes may have been free, but we've paid dearly for everything else."

There is a fine line between making sport of the opposition and taking a cheap shot. Some of Spurrier's critics in the media felt maybe he had crossed that boundary.

On the other hand, those who knew Spurrier best were also aware he was charting a course for himself and his team where he could never turn back--perhaps on purpose.

And that he was trying to gain a measure of retribution for constantly being told that FSU was signing most of the good high school players in the state.

Those words would come back to haunt the Gator coach, not once, but twice during the season. For little did Spurrier realize he would have to face his nemesis from Tallahassee on two different occasions.

Among the weirdest of projections you could have made, you could have never predicted that Florida and Florida State would play a doubleheader--first on Nov. 26 in Tallahassee and again Jan. 2 in the USF&G Sugar Bowl.

But, then, there have been few Gator football seasons as weird as 1994's.

All the while, Spurrier had done nothing to discourage his team's lofty advance billing. The Gator offense was expected to be every bit as explosive as it had always been (Spurrier's teams lead the SEC every year in total yards).

And, if we could believe all the press clippings from 1994 spring camp, Spurrier's defense was also vastly improved under new coordinator Bob Pruett.

There was plenty of reason for optimism.

Under Spurrier, Florida had not only overcome its beleaguered reputation as an NCAA punching bag, but prospered while serving out the sentence.

After four years, Spurrier had already elevated the Gator football program to new horizon. In his first season, Florida went 9-2 and Spurrier was named SEC coach of the Year.

The Gators had the best record in the SEC, but weren't eligible for the trophy. That 1990 team would always have a special place in its coach's heart and he would never forget them.

Spurrier was on a roll as the '94 season began. In addition to winning two conference titles in the last three years and having his last three teams finish among the Associated Press Top Ten elite, Spurrier had, up until 1994:

■Compiled the best four-year conference record (27-5) of any SEC school and the best in school history (39-10).

■Won 11 games for the first time in Florida history and nine or more games four years straight.

■Had his team ranked in the AP poll 66 of the first 67 weeks that he'd coached the Gators.

As the Gators took the field against lowly New Mexico State on Saturday, Sept. 3, the conventional thinking was that a 35 or 40-point win would keep them atop the polls.

As it turned out, it could have easily been a 100-point win had Spurrier chosen not to show mercy on the lowly Aggies.

On Florida's first eight possessions, quarterback Terry Dean tied a national record by throwing seven touchdown passes, four of them to wide receiver Jack Jackson.

That one half of football was going to have a negative impact on the relationship of Spurrier and Dean before the season was over.

Dean was on the bench with five minutes left in the second quarter. At halftime, Dean and Jackson were wearing street clothes.

Despite suffering a slight injury to his foot in the first quarter, Dean had still managed to throw for touchdowns five, six and seven.

Final score: Florida 70, New Mexico State 21.

The reaction of Florida coaches and fans was mixed, with some concern about the secondary, which had given up long strikes for touchdowns on coverage mistakes.

"That's just a bad individual play by a couple of our guys over there in the secondary," Spurrier said, not wanting to sound ungrateful for the convincing win.

Still, the defense had not been dominant as expected under new defensive coordinator Bob Pruett.

As for the fact that Dean had tied a long-time NCAA passing record with seven touchdowns, Spurrier said:

"We're not real excited about setting records against an opponent that's not up to the caliber of most teams we play."

The mission had been accomplished and the Spurrier juggernaut would need to be finely tuned as the Southeastern Conference schedule started next week: Kentucky in "The Swamp," with a trip to Vols Country in Knoxville the following Saturday.

Dress rehearsal for The Big Show was over and the reviews were quite good. Opening night jitters were out of the way and the Spurrier Express appeared right on schedule.

This No. 1 thing just didn't take hold. Nobody said much about it. A few tee-shirts were sold. The fans didn't seem to catch on to their inherent bragging rights to which they were now entitled.

"I never heard our fans shout 'We're No. 1!'" Spurrier said all in fun after the New Mexico game, mocking anger.

"Maybe they didn't know how to do it. Where were our cheerleaders? I thought they were going to yell it? In the fourth quarter some little group over in the corner tried to get it going and everybody I guess had gone home or gone to sleep. If we're fortunate enough to be there next week, maybe somebody can teach them."

Too late. The next day the Associated Press and the CNN/USA Today polls revealed a huge surprise: Florida had dropped to No. 2, just behind Nebraska, which hadn't played a game that week.

Winning your home opener by 49 points apparently just wasn't impressive enough. Spurrier made light of the poll "demotion" the next week, saying it wasn't all that important.

"My athletic director (Jeremy Foley) said it was my fault," Spurrier joked. "He said we should have won by *fifty*."

And so the horse race in the "Poll Bowl" was on, with Florida opening up an early favorite, charging out of the gate and dropping back a length at the first pole, or poll. There was just no way to figure the logic of these pollsters.

The question was, how much did it matter, being ranked No. 2 that early? And if you couldn't hold your serve after winning your opener by 49, what kind of rules were they playing by?

A larger question than that lingered, however: In the end, how much would the polls really matter to the Gators?

V. Spurrier almost wasn't the coach

There really was no grand plan for Steve Spurrier to become a coach of any kind, let alone Florida's savior.

After more than a decade of knocking around the San Francisco Forty Niners as a reserve quarterback and punter and eventually winding up as the starter for the ill-fated Tampa Bay Bucs in their inaugural season and then getting cut by Denver and failing to stick with Miami, Spurrier returned home to Gainesville in 1977 to ponder his future.

"I really hadn't established any kind of track record as a coach," Spurrier recalled. "I had come out of the NFL and I wasn't sure what I wanted to do. I was just hanging around, playing a lot of golf. I thought I'd have enough money left over from pro ball to just play golf and have some kind of PR job. . .the way most guys do when their playing days are over."

At that point, coaching was not paramount to him. Then one day he decided to start attending Gator games, sitting in the stands for the first time in his life. It was then he first realized, "how important this game of football is to so many people."

It was as a spectator the idea first occurred to him that he might coach.

'At Duke, Spurrier had to advertise in the school newspaper for receivers.'

"I thought coaching was something you could get your teeth into and could be fun. Obviously we all want to do something in life that doesn't seem like work."

Shortly thereafter Spurrier was hired as Doug Dickey's assistant to help coach Florida quarterbacks. And, in fact, Spurrier called the plays late in the season. But after a 4-7 campaign, Dickey was fired. So it was on to Georgia Tech.

Spurrier's backfield coach from college, Pepper Rodgers, was head coach at Tech, where Spurrier would get a chance to expand on his play-calling prowess the next season.

Rodgers was about to be fired. In Atlanta, Spurrier ran into Duke had coach Red Wilson while on a high school recruiting trip and was offered the job as Blue Devils offensive coordinator.

It began to look like Spurrier was a bad-luck charm for head coaches.

At Duke, Spurrier had to advertise in the school newspaper for wide receivers. The Blue Devils went 2-9. But the new offensive coordinator began cranking up his offense to record-setting levels in the Atlantic Coast Conference and attracted attention. And with the help of some semi-anonymous players, Wilson and his young coordinator began to turn things around.

When he looks back on his second season as an assistant at Duke, Spurrier fondly remembers Ron Salley, a name that you won't find in the Blue Devils' hall of fame. It was Salley, now an attorney in Los Angeles, who came off the bench and led his team back from a 24-15 deficit to a 29-24 victory over Virginia which was crucial in preserving the season and launching the Duke turnaround.

Salley's heroics came at a time when his team needed them, as starting quarterback Ben Bennett was out with injury. "Ron led us on a couple of 80-yard drives," said Spurrier, "and we came back to win after we had started the season 0-2. We went on to win five more games and go 6-5."

To this day, Spurrier and Salley exchange letters almost every year.

Duke was back on a winning track and in his third year, Spurrier was still setting offensive records. Spurrier helped the Devils to another 6-5 season. During this time, he was also experimenting with secret offensive weapons: The hidden ball trick, the Emory and Henry formation, the no-huddle offense.

These would surface again in later years.

One of the people who noticed Spurrier's fertile imagination was millionaire John Bassett, a *very* impulsive, *very* rich man and a risk-taker.

Bassett flew to Durham to interview Spurrier.

After an excellent conversation and an even better T-bone steak at Hartman's, he offered Steve the job as head coach of the Tampa Bay Bandits. He took the position without blinking or ever even discussing salary.

At 37, Spurrier would become the youngest head coach in pro football. And he gave them offensive football like they'd never seen it in the pros, including all the stuff he discovered in his X's and O's laboratory at Duke--the no-huddle offense, Emory and Henry, etc.

Which, of course, others eventually stole.

Successful though he may be, Spurrier realizes there's only the tiniest of margins between that and failure. "I feel thankful everyday for just a few things that happened along the way. There were some very key victories, and most of them happened in my career at Duke," he said.

All the while, the fate of Gator football was riding a roller-coaster in the eighties, from an SEC championship to NCAA probation.

Spurrier often told his friends he didn't think he'd ever be the head coach of the Gators because "I don't think the job will ever be open while I'm coaching."

That's what he told me one January night in 1986 in Mobile, Alabama. The USFL had decided to challenge the NFL through the courts for the right to play in the fall, but chose to go on hiatus in the process. Spurrier had just released his Bandit coaches and although he was still on the team's payroll, Spurrier's career was very much in doubt.

After a couple of beers that night, I drove Steve back to his hotel and we sat in front with the motor running while we talked about his future.

It mystified me as to why this talented young coach wasn't being hotly pursued by some athletic director in search of a fresh face. And why the University of Florida, instead of turning over the reins to Hall, wouldn't first look to its own.

"I think Galen will do a good job for them and he'll be there for a long time," Spurrier told me. "Maybe it's just as well. Going back to Gainesville where I have so many friends might not be the best thing."

Frankly, I believe Spurrier may have worried--with some justification--that he wouldn't be able to live up to the legendary status he had built up as a player.

Fortunately for Spurrier, Steve Sloan resigned at Duke and went to Alabama, so it was back to Durham and Duke, this time as the head coach.

"That was the only opportunity I had back in 1987," Spurrier recalled. "We were 35-19 with the Bandits, but I didn't have a whole lot of people coming after me to hire me. I had a reputation of playing too much golf and not working to hard."

How uncanny that Spurrier would go to Duke and reach the pinnacle of his success at the precise moment things were turning sour for Hall and his football team.

After losing his opener to Ole Miss, Hall's '89 team won four straight and it looked, as Spurrier had said, like Galen was solidified in that job. I certainly thought so.

I had resigned from *The Denver Post* and moved to Ponte Vedra, Florida, where I covered most of the Gator games for *The Florida Times-Union.*

Taking Spurrier at his word and accepting that he'd never be a candidate at Florida, I wrote a column suggesting that perhaps Florida should extend Hall's contract.

A friend of mine with connections to the inner-workings of the Florida athletic department--Jacksonville attorney Gene Peek--warned me not to make any bold predictions about Hall's longevity. I should have listened.

News of the NCAA investigation was ongoing, but it didn't seem to seriously implicate Hall.

Two days later, Hall resigned and defensive coordinator Gary Darnell took over as interim. The hunt was on for the next Florida coach and all eyes turned to Durham, North Carolina where Spurrier's Blue Devils were about to win the Atlantic Coast Conference and to go their first bowl in two decades.

Unbelievably, however, there was an undercurrent of resistance about Spurrier, not the least of which came from Athletic Director Bill Arnsparger, although he later denied that. It was Arnsparger, along with interim president Robert Bryan and athletic board member Nick Cassissi, who flew to North Carolina and offered Spurrier the job.

Much of the credit for the enthusiasm to hire Spurrier must be given to Bryan, who went on a mission to land him as Hall's successor. The fact is, however, that Arnsparger was slow on arriving at the conclusion Spurrier was the right man when almost everyone else was so positive about him.

According to a source close to the athletic department, Cassissi and Bryan accompanied Arnsparger to make certain he tendered the proper offer. The suspicion was that Arnsparger didn't want to hire anybody who might rally the alumni or detract from his influence or dilute the power of the athletic director.

Or even that Arnsparger wanted the coaching job himself.

For better or worse, politics has always played a big role in the Florida football program. Governors and senators often had a hand in the hiring and firing of coaches. There was a strong political tide running in favor of Spurrier, but Arnsparger apparently felt he could stem it.

Yet one of the reasons for Arnsparger's power base was that he had been assigned the task by embarrassed state politicians and university administrators of cleaning up the program and ridding it of unsavory characters.

So Arnsparger became a kind of self-appointed sheriff.

One fall day on the Riverwalk in Jacksonville I had lunch with Arsnparger to ask about his coaching search.

This was long after Spurrier's name had been introduced in practically every sports column in the state as Florida's most desirable and most viable candidate--including my own, ad nauseam. I asked Arnsparger about his leading candidates. Incredibly, he remarked: "I still think there's a bright young assistant coach out there somewhere."

Arnsparger was guilty of one of he following:

1)Lying about Spurrier so as to throw us off the track (I doubt that);

Or, 2)Ignorant about Spurrier's true coaching ability;

Or, 3)Wanted to coach the team himself.

When Spurrier was hired on Dec. 31, the press conference was turned into a veritable love feast.

Instead of admitting his doubts, Arnsparger said he really felt he had landed the best possible man for the job. I knew better because Arnsparger had told me differently.

Two days later, after taking the Gator mantle, Spurrier got a commitment from his first player: Quarterback Terry Dean of Naples, who had originally hoped to play for Auburn, where his father, Frank, had once attended.

Once Spurrier hit the ground running and started winning, the healing process began and not even Bill Arsnparger would dare step in front of this fast-moving Spurrier Express.

So unpopular had Arnsparger become during the previous NCAA investigation because of his Gestapo-like tactics under the guise of what he called "compliance" that his power base began to erode. He seemed to sensed that his coup attempt had failed, so, not surprisingly, Arnsparger eventually stepped down.

In his late sixties, Arnsparger went back into coaching as the Chargers' defensive coordinator, retiring after his team lost to the 49ers in Super Bowl XXIX.

Hardly anybody--most of all, Arnsparger--could have imagined what spectacular windfall would result from the hiring of Spurrier. It was, in fact, the pivotal point in Florida football history in the most critical of times. He may have been the only person who could have saved Florida football in this crisis.

So Sir Lancelot from the house of Duke arrived in just the nick of time.

Considering what Spurrier has accomplished in his first five years, on the heels of NCAA sanctions, Florida has been blessed with one of the most dramatic turnarounds in college football history.

Giving his predecessors, Charley Pell and Galen Hall, full credit for his impressive winning record, Spurrier still easily surpassed the U-F's most productive eras in five years.

The Pell-Hall team of 1984 finished No. 1 in polls by the New York Times and Sporting News, technically meaning they won a "National Championship" of sorts. Hall wound up as the '84 coach, winning his last eight games and clinching the school's first SEC title, but it was taken away because of NCAA sanctions.

The Pell-Hall era of 1983-85 produced three teams that finished among the nation's top six in the Associated Press poll and a record of 27-4-3 (83.8 per cent), second best in the country. But, from 1984 to 1990, Florida was also on probation twice.

After five seasons, Spurrier's winning percentage was only a hair behind that torrid pace (79.8 per cent , just 2 1/2 victories shy). His teams finished ranked in the Top Ten four seasons, from 1991-94.

Even though the 1990 Gators weren't eligible to win the SEC, they finished with the best record. And they've won the title three of the last four seasons.

The fact that Spurrier would accomplished all that--without once ever getting his hands slapped or even the remotest hint of an investigation--does two things:

1)Makes you wonder why there had to be a cheating scandal in the first place;

2)Makes you wonder why Florida--or somebody--didn't come calling for Spurrier a lot sooner than 1989.

It also makes you wonder where the Florida football program would be without imports from Tennessee. Spurrier was the fourth coach since 1950 with some tie to the Volunteer State. (Gloating Tennesseans take note: Though Spurrier was reared in East Tennessee, he was actually born in Miami Beach, Florida.)

So those wonderful people who brought you the Grand Ol' Opry, Dollywood and world class walking horses were ready to help again when Florida needed a makeover. This time Tennessee would provide Florida with the greatest coach in its football history.

VI. life in 'The Swamp' with a No. 1 ranking

Florida Field has evolved into truly one of the magnificent college football venues, hot and humid and loud, perpetuating a mystique much like Tiger Stadium in Baton Rouge back when LSU ruled the SEC under Paul Dietzel.

Home field advantage at "The Swamp," as it has been dubbed since Spurrier arrived in 1990, has become huge for the Gators. "Snake Pit" might have been a more appropriate name, because the visiting team often gets bitten.

There in that oval, excavated from the Central Florida soil at about sea level, Spurrier still works his magic in an almost mystical fashion, as he has always done both as a coach and a player.

After five years as coach, Spurrier had lost only there twice in 29 games.

It was on the natural turf of Florida Field, *before* it was co-named "Ben Hill Griffin Stadium" after the rich Central Florida philanthropist, that Spurrier's extraordinary individual exploits won him the Heisman Trophy.

Spurrier was an incredible college football player, one of the most exciting ever to snap on his chin-strap, a cunning competitor with a surplus of guile and imagination.

'Spurrier was an incredible college football player. . .'

He invented ways to win football games in pressure situations.

Even though he never achieved that same level in the NFL, for three years he was easily one of the most exciting players in the game.

Little wonder, then, that when he took the job in 1990, one of the first things Spurrier requested was that the artificial turf be ripped up and replaced by natural grass, the same kind of surface upon which he had reigned supreme as a player and established so many milestones.

Definitely, Florida Field has become a hostile environment for outsiders. Every game now is a sellout and Spurrier's success has re-energized Gator fans. The crowds hover oppressively over the playing field, which sits below like a drained lake, or, Swamp.

The noise of the exuberant spectators is amplified by the bowl-like underground amphitheater.

"That's one reason we named it 'The Swamp,'" said Assistant Athletic Director Norm Carlson, who teamed up with Spurrier to provide the nickname. "It used to be a drainage area and it sits down here in a hole like it was a Swamp. Steve wanted some kind of name like 'Death Valley' at Clemson. So we settled on 'The Swamp.'"

They come in droves, they yell loud and they dress loud, mostly in leisurely attire. Gone are the days when Florida fans put on a sport coat or dress to attend a Gator football game. Some fans have re-defined the term "casual."

It's probably just a perception, but it seems they lead the world in the variety of orange and blue paraphernalia which they don for home games.

Admittedly, some of it looks like it came out of the K-Mart basement, but you can also find some women decked out in fancy-schmancy beaded tops that cost over $150.

And tons of T-shirts. One shirt totally unrelated to Florida that caught my eye bore the inscription: "Help! I'm talking and I can't shut up!"

One passerby wanted to know if she had bought that for Spurrier, who by now was gaining a reputation as a hip-shooter and a guy who often spoke his mind.

From whence came all this color? When Charley Pell came to Florida from Clemson in 1979 he noticed that school colors weren't often flown or worn with great dignity and pride. So he set about to change all that through the admonition for Gator fans to wear their orange and blue proudly. It stuck and has become a tradition.

Thus Florida Field was becoming a sea, or Swamp, of orange and blue. Especially as the stadium grew larger. With the North end zone closed in and double-decked, Ben Hill Griffin Stadium bulges to over 85,000 every Saturday.

Not much attention is paid to this stat anymore, but Florida's attendance, consistently among the nation's top 10, has become one of the true success stories in college sports.

Think about this: In a state that boasts two NFL franchises and was about to get a third, plus three of the best college teams in America, the Gators had consistently drawn the biggest football crowds in Florida.

There is still some class distinction among Gator fans, the *old money* and the *nouveau*. The latter is most likely not a Florida native or Florida graduate, just started attending games in the nineties, tends to be more vocal and quite often crassly boorish and overly-critical.

Now that Spurrier has the Gators back on top, it has become hip for the *nouveau* fans to whine excessively, as if they have earned that right. *Old money* fans wonder where they were when Georgia was clubbing Florida 51-0 in the rain. Back when a 5-5 record was respectable.

By Game 2 in 1994, they were all atwitter. Now, with Kentucky next on the schedule, many of them whined about not being ranked No. 1 in the nation anymore.

Though a pronounced underdog, the Wildcats had beaten Louisville 21-14 just the Saturday before and had nearly knocked off the Gators in Lexington the year before.

In 1993, walk-on receiver Chris Doering caught a desperation touchdown pass from quarterback Danny Wuerffel on the play as the Gators "stole one," according to Spurrier, 24-20.

The call of Gator broadcaster Mick Hubert captured the surprise of the moment: *"Doering's got a touchdown! Doering's got a touchdown! On my! Doering's got a touchdown! Unbelievable! Chris Doering got a touchdown!"*

And Florida got a victory to advance toward the SEC Championship game in 1993 which the Gators would win. Florida owned Kentucky of late: Seven straight wins over the Wildcats, including the last four by Spurrier.

It's hard to believe that Kentucky had once regularly pummeled the Gators in both basketball and football back in the late forties and early fifties. Maybe that's a good history lesson for Gator fans in the post-Spurrier era.

This being the first SEC game of the year, nothing could be taken for granted. Was Florida's offense really that potent, or had New Mexico State's defense simply been that bad? And if Spurrier turned loose Terry Dean, Jack Jackson and the Fab Four Freshmen--Elijah Williams, Fred Taylor, Ike Hilliard and Reidel Anthony--how badly could they beat up on Kentucky?

It's a well documented fact that Spurrier never apologizes for his team scoring excessively and does not believe in discouraging scrubs from trying to crack the end zone. He is in the business of teaching offense and nothing is to be learned by holding back.

He is also in the business of getting his team ranked as highly as possible and that comes about only by overwhelming your opponent.

"Somebody asked my athletic director, Tom Butters, at Duke what he thought about his coach running up the score," Spurrier said.

"And Tom said, 'I think it's great! I love it! Can you imagine somebody accusing the coach at Duke of running up the score!'"

There was also a lesson to be learned about killer instinct, about putting you opponent away when you've got him down. Later in the year, Spurrier's "get-all-you-can-when-you-can" philosophy would prove to be infinite wisdom. Because against FSU the Gators found out the hard way that even a 28-point lead in the fourth quarter isn't safe.

Spurrier had chosen to approach the Kentucky game cautiously, though confidently. Not even he could have guessed that his team would be so dominant of Bill Curry's Wildcats.

SEC teams just can't seem to penetrate "The Swamp's" mystique, which is another reason the Gators were the pre-season conference favorite: Home field advantage.

The only question that would remain after the Kentucky game was just how powerful a team Spurrier could field. Answer: Very powerful. The hapless Kentucky Wildcats would fall victim to what could possibly be a dynasty in the making.

Writers and broadcasters close to the Florida program were beginning to suspect this Gator team might slowly be developing into the best in school history, maybe even better than the Pell-Hall 1984 bunch (which a special media panel voted as the "Greatest Gator Team" for this book.)

The Gators' offensive firepower quickly over-ran an out-manned Wildcat defense.

And a new star was born under the Spurrier regime: Red-shirt freshman Elijah "Eli" Williams from Milton in the panhandle of Florida.

It didn't take Eli long to start working on the records.

He had fallen just four yards short of 100 yards rushing against New Mexico State in his debut on a day when he was so nervous that he almost couldn't keep his food down.

Williams ran for 115 yards on 13 carries against Kentucky, including a 51-yarder, the longest ever by a Gator back playing for Spurrier. And the defense proved a little more noteworthy, allowing Kentucky just seven points.

Williams was one half of the freshman tailback tandem which Spurrier hoped would become the centerpiece of his running game over the next four years.

Fred Taylor, a 6-1, 214-pounder from Belle Glade High School in South Florida, rushed for 72 yards against New Mexico State, scoring his first touchdown. After having been red-shirted for a year, it wasn't necessarily good news to Williams that he would have to share time with Taylor.

This would prove to be a wise decision by Spurrier, because he would need them both. And they proved to be a compatible one-two punch.

The Gator defense was blessed with the best front four in college football--Kevin Carter, Henry McMillian, Ellis Johnson and Mark Campbell. But it recorded no sacks against Kentucky, and that was beginning to concern Bob Pruett.

Oddly enough, Spurrier found himself explaining away the victory, saying he hoped his team could "get over a big win" without becoming overconfident for Tennessee.

He said he had hoped that the game would wind up in the neighborhood of 31-7, but "it sort of got out of hand."

Although his fourth string quarterback, Brian Schottenheimer, was throwing touchdown passes to players not even listed on the depth chart, a few brows were furrowed about the 73-7 spanking of his SEC peer, Bill Curry.

What had he said to Curry after the game?

"The same thing I say to all of them. 'Nice game,'" Spurrier remarked rather coolly.

Oh yes. About Terry's Dean's quest for the Heisman Trophy? On the heels of that SEC record-setting and NCAA record-tying night of seven touchdown passes against New Mexico State in just a quarter and a half, he played a little over a half against the Wildcats and threw for four more TDs.

Dean now led the nation in touchdown passes with 11. But it's hard to be a serious Heisman Trophy candidate when you play only half the game because your team is so far ahead. And when your coach tells you to get dressed in street clothes at the half.

Dean's success so early would later prove to be an Achilles heel for Spurrier, who was hoping to keep the focus off of individuals.

The No. 1 thing died down some, although some fans tried to get the post-game chant going. Spurrier seemed to be having fun with it.

"They should have been cheering 'we're No. 2,'" Spurrier said jokingly. He then stated that Nebraska deserved the No. 1 ranking, that his Gators really hadn't done all that much to deserve it.

One got the feeling that Spurrier was playing coy. He was taking his team to his home state of Tennessee the next week and that hadn't been a very pleasurable experience in recent years. "Hopefully we're up to the challenge," he said. "We haven't done very well up there in recent years."

Suddenly the "conspiracy" came to light. Dropping to the No. 2 position was no accident, it was a PLOT! Some of the veteran Gator fans who had been through this land of broken dreams too many times before figured out that when nobody was looking, these devious pollsters had gone and stolen the national championship right from under their noses.

The Gators' collective conscience seemed to be whispering:

Here we go again: They'll do anything and everything to deprive us of the national championship that we so richly deserve. It doesn't happen to Notre Dame, Miami or Florida State. Just to the Florida Gators because they want to dump on us again.

The conspiracy theory is easily sold to Gator fans. Like my former classmate and football teammate at Ocala High School, Richard Barber, always said: "How come the Gators are always on the WRONG side of making history?"

Although the head coach kept insisting that being ranked No. 1 wasn't important--and he honestly made a good point about it being too early in the season--Spurrier obviously hadn't been aware of this *Clear And Present Danger:*

If both Nebraska and Florida won the remainder of their games, they likely would stay in their 1-2 positions, so the Cornhuskers had the upper hand at the top of both polls at the moment.

The Big Eight winner was bound for the Federal Express Orange Bowl, the SEC champion to the USF&G Sugar Bowl, the Big Ten to the Rose. So unless the Gators finished the season undefeated, how would they have a chance for a national title?

There was good news on the way. The AP poll would have Florida No. 1. Thus began the five-week reign of the Gators atop the national polls. Now that they were back there, how would they react? No matter, if Florida didn't win the SEC title, there would be no chance, anyway. And going to Knoxville was not exactly a stroll in the park.

VII. tracing the roots to Davey Crockett

Despite the coaching shuttle between Gainesville and Knoxville and the interchangeable part, the Tennessee-Florida series lacked real tradition. The two schools had only played each other 23 times-- just seven since World War II. Only four of those games were played in the nineties while Spurrier was coaching the Gators. And during Spurrier's era, until 1994, the home team had always won.

Little wonder, then, that though somewhat young, the Florida-Tennessee rivalry quickly became a bitter one during the nineties because of all the interaction among coaches. Little wonder, too, that when Spurrier brought his high-powered, turbo-jet offense to Neyland Stadium in September 1994, they were mounting anti-aircraft guns in the Smokies.

With the Gators in their sights, the talk show callers in Tennessee starting shooting at Spurrier early in the week.

One caller to a Knoxville station said he'd like to see his beloved Vols win by at least 100-0. Payback.

The consensus of the callers was that the uppity ex-patriate from that hedonist state of Florida should be punished for his self indulgence.

'Find A Place In Your Heart For Steve Spurrier. . .'

(Namely because Spurrier ran the score up on these poor innocent rascals. See Florida 70, New Mexico 21 and Florida 73, Kentucky 7).

Another caller accused Spurrier of whining about officiating and criticized him for poor sportsmanship in flinging his golf visor to the ground.

Not everybody in Tennessee was totally blinded by prejudice, however. This particular Knoxville talk show host ultimately refused to embrace all this Spurrier bashing, finally retorting: "But you've got to give Steve Spurrier credit. He's going to beat you as badly as he can and not apologize for it. He's got courage. He doesn't care what you say about him, and he doesn't care about what's going to happen next year when he plays you again."

In his own way, that announcer probably came as close to defining Spurrier, the coach, as anybody all season.

Others had fun with it. A Knoxville sports columnist wrote that the over/under on Spurrier's visor-flinging was 6 and if he flung it more than that Florida would probably lose. *News-Sentinel* sports columnist John Adams felt compelled to give due recognition to one of the state's favorite sons.

After all, Spurrier was boasting the No. 1 ranked team in the nation (Associated Press), and Adams suggested that Steve was the best thing to happen to the Tennessee-Florida rivalry since the Hatfields met up with the McCoys.

The headline on Adams' column Friday, Sept. 16, read: "Find A Place In Your Heart For Spurrier." And Adams used an editor's note for a disclaimer, warning Vols fans that if they had a violent reaction to praise of Spurrier, perhaps they should "see your therapist."

Speaking about all those short-sighted athletic directors and NFL owners who passed over Spurrier, Adams wrote:

Spurrier couldn't make it to the final round of interviews for the head-coaching job LSU eventually gave to Mike Archer. His success with Tampa Bay of the USFL couldn't convince the late Hugh Culverhouse that Spurrier could do as much for his battered NFL Bucs.

The consensus among the football establishment was that Spurrier liked golf and a good time more than he liked coaching and recruiting. Even some of his friends wondered if he had the necessary work ethic to succeed as head coach. And maybe at one time he didn't.

Maybe the slights--real or imagined--had driven him where he might not have otherwise gone. He's already on his way to becoming the best coach in college football.

And he has already done as much for the Tennessee-Florida rivalry as the SEC's divisional realignment and Doug Dickey, who graduated from Florida, came to UT as head football coach, and returned to UT as athletic director."

Spurrier did like golf and still does. He does like to laugh and cajole and drink some beer with his friends. And he doesn't think you have to stay in the film room for days, or sleep over in your office. He is a nineties kind of coach who prides himself on working smart instead of hard just to prove his work ethic.

Tennessee fans should remind Gator fans how lucky they are to have Spurrier. Gator fans should lift their glasses high in honor of the Volunteer State, which has been a primary breeding ground for Gator coaches and players.

It all started with Neyland, who begat Ray Graves and Bob Woodruff. And then Woodruff begat Doug Dickey. And between Graves and Dickey they begat Spurrier, who begat Florida's halcyon days. So there's a whole lot of Davey Crockett coonskin down in "The Swamp."

If you wanted to coach football at Florida, you'd have a better chance if you passed through Tennessee first. Because much of college football in the South can be traced back in some way to the Volunteer State or Gen. Bob Neyland, the militaristic defensive mastermind.

Neyland coached the Vols in 1928 and beat Florida's best-ever team to that point.

In a battle of two unbeaten teams that year, Florida went into Knoxville with eight straight wins, leading the nation in scoring and a rock-solid defense that had allowed no more than one touchdown to each opponent.

If the '28 Gators could knock off the 8-0-1 Vols, they would win the Southern Conference title and perhaps gain a Rose Bowl bid.

On a bitter cold day in Knoxville, Florida had an extra point blocked and lost 13-12. Neyland was said to coach from a wheel chair that day, but it was also rumored that he was "suddenly cured" after the victory and was so inspired that he rose up out of the chair.

The Gators went coach-hunting often following World War II and Tennessee was a happy hunting ground. The two Southeastern Conference schools apparently have established some sort of free trade agreement on athletic directors and coaches, with Florida usually coming out ahead on the trades.

Two former Tennessee players and one former Vols coach have come to Florida as head coaches. At least one former Gator player or coach has been head coach or athletic director at UT.

And the most decorated player in Florida history, Spurrier, was a Tennessee schoolboy who became Florida's most successful head coach.

Gruff-talking Bob Woodruff started it all.

Though he finally was banished from Gainesville for his conservative offense and his third down punts, ex-Tennessee player and Neyland disciple Woodruff did bring respectability and fiscal responsibility to Florida in the fifties.

Nobody can ever say that Woodruff didn't build a solid defense and a strong administrative staff in the athletic department when his 10-year regime began in 1950. And his 1952 team played in the Gators' first-ever bowl, winding up with a No. 15 national ranking.

There wasn't much money in college programs after World War II and very little funding for Florida.

Woodruff came up with the idea of incorporating the athletic department apart from the university and persuading greyhound track operators to hold a charitable day for Gator athletics, one of the keys to upgrading talent and facilities. It was an ingenious decision and profitable move for Florida athletics.

If Bob Woodruff had understood the importance of a wide-open offense like he understood the bottom line in finance, they might have built a statue of him in Gainesville.

What ultimately cost Woodruff his job at Florida was the decision to run out the clock with the ball at mid-field and the score tied at 13-13 with Rice in 1959. And the inability to sell his decision to the alumni. His feeble comment was: "Well, I'll gamble to win, but never to lose."

Though fired, Woodruff wound up back at Tennessee as Athletic Director where he later hired his former Florida quarterback, Doug Dickey, as coach. Together, they flourished. And, ironically, Dickey would one day return to coach at his alma mater in Gainesville and then to Knoxville where he would succeed Woodruff as athletic director.

The man who followed Woodruff to Gainesville was also an ex-Vol player. Former Tennessee and Philadelphia Eagles lineman Ray Graves was actually a member of Bobby Dodd's staff at Georgia Tech with a defensive bent.

Graves arrived in Gainesville determined not to repeat Woodruff's mistake, promising he'd never punt on third down. And he brought with him a former Tech quarterback with a wild offensive imagination, Pepper Rodgers.

Graves wasted no time in keeping his promise to take off the wraps. In his third game as head coach against his old boss, Bobby Dodd, Graves elected to go for two points and the Gators upset the favored Yellow Jackets, 18-17, on a glorious day at Florida Field.

I've always contended that one play bought Graves a decade of good will with alumni. Graves agrees with that. "But it was an easy decision to make," said Graves. "We didn't even deliberate about it on the sideline."

After a strong start in the early sixties, Graves went out and got himself a world-class passer, another hill child from East Tennessee. Nobody, including Graves, knew just exactly how he had secured the future of the Gators with the issuance of that one scholarship to Spurrier.

Who could have guessed back in 1963 that Spurrier would not only become the school's first and only Heisman Trophy 30 years later, but also the first coach to win a legitimate SEC title?

I asked Graves to relate one more time why and how he had recruited Spurrier to Florida.

"My brother, Edwin, was the postmaster in Knoxville, Tennessee," said Graves. "Steve's team (Science Hill of Johnson City) was playing Knoxville Central and Edwin went out to see the game. He called me and said, 'Ray, this Steve Spurrier does everything--punts, passes, kick extra points. You better check him out."

It came down to Florida and Ole Miss. On his visit to the Florida campus, Graves squired his new recruit around and gave him personal attention. Already an accomplished athlete in football, basketball and baseball--"I was probably best in basketball," says Spurrier--the kid from Johnson City told Graves he was considering taking up golf.

"The university had just bought a golf course," recalled Graves. "So I took him out there and let him hit a couple of buckets of balls. So help me, I think to this day that may have helped him make up his mind about Florida."

No coach ever won more games than Graves at Florida (70), although Spurrier will soon be closing in on that record. He took his teams to five bowls, winning four, but the Gators of that era never could win a championship of any kind.

Yet until Spurrier's teams of the nineties and the Pell/Hall teams of the mid eighties, no coach had even reached the milestone that Graves' sophomore-laden 1969 team did with a 9-1-1 mark.

A team, incidentally, that began the season with a bang, as sophomore quarterback John Reaves hit sophomore wide receiver Carlos Alvarez with a bomb on the game's third play and the Gators smacked down the No. 1 ranked Houston Cougars, 59-34, in the season opener.

The most incredible aspect of that 1969 record is that it still didn't save Graves' job. Because of a back-room political deal struck before the season began in which Graves had secretly agreed to move upstairs to the athletic director's job, Florida actually changed coaches on the heels of its best football record in history after the '69 season.

The new coach was Dickey--the same quarterback for Bob Woodruff in the early fifties. Dickey was a member of perhaps the school's most famous backfield to that date--at least in the T-formation era. The fullback in 1953 was Rick Casares, later to become an All-Pro fullback for the Chicago Bears.

Casares actually started the season at quarterback and played three games there before Dickey was brought in as the "field general" and Fred Robinson came in to spell Dickey on passing downs. The halfbacks were Jay (Papa) Hall, a gifted athlete and SEC high jump champion, and Buford Long, drafted by the New York Giants.

The starting quarterback was to have been Haywood Sullivan, but the Red Sox signed him for a handsome $75,000 bonus and Sullivan skipped his senior year.

Sullivan's decision proved to be a good one, as he went on to become the Red Sox catcher, general manager and, eventually, one of their owners.

It was not so good for Woodruff's Florida team, which, without Sullivan, posted a 3-5-2 record.

Ironically, before arriving in his new job, Dickey's 1969 SEC co-champion Vols team was beaten in the Gator Bowl by Graves' Gators, 14-13, in what had to be one of the most bizarre pairings in history.

When Dickey resigned his job as head coach at Tennessee, accepting the Gators' offer to return home to Gainesville, it shocked many people, especially the Vols backers who had watched him restore their program to dignity.

It also shocked most everybody associated with the Florida program.

Most Gator players felt they had been betrayed. All-American wide receiver Alvarez considered transferring, but later changed his mind. The move also angered some Florida fans who felt that Graves' defensive coordinator Gene Ellenson should be his successor.

The clandestine nature of the switch also drew the attention of the NCAA, which investigated the program for "breach of ethics" because the Florida administration had lied about the change.

Dickey's era promised so much and delivered so little. In the mid-seventies he finally achieved a modicum of success with 8-4, 9-3, 8-4 records. But a 6-4 and 4-7 took him down after the 1978 season, never having equaled or surpassed Graves' record of 9-1-1 in his last year.

Ironically, when Dickey was fired in 1978, so was a young former NFL quarterback in his rookie season as an assistant: Steve Spurrier.

Before Spurrier would become Florida's 19th head coach on Dec. 31, 1989, there were two more go-betweens, neither of whom, believe it or not, came from Tennessee:

Pell (Alabama) and Hall (Penn State) brought much honor to Gainesville, but they would also depart ignominiously.

Pell, coming from Clemson as head coach, was the first to fall. After coaching the Gators to a 9-2-1 mark in 1983, he resigned in disgrace three games deep into 1984 over trouble with the NCAA and refused to pin any of the rap on anybody but himself. Florida went on probation.

Pell later failed in business and suffered from bouts of depression which caused him to attempt suicide and at the writing of this book was working to clear his name and get another crack at coaching.

Following a new spate of NCAA charges five years later, Hall, a former assistant to Barry Switzer at Oklahoma, was fired after five games in 1989. Defensive coordinator Gary Darnell took over as interim the last seven games as the Gators went 7-5. Florida was subsequently put on probation again and--depending on whom you chose to believe--may have come perilously close to suffering the dreaded "death penalty."

What followed was a sorry episode in the school's history.

In the name of "compliance" under the NCAA mandate to clean up its cheating scandal or face extermination, school administrators and politicians went on a witch hunt.

The once-proud University of Florida athletic program was in the sewer. For the third time since 1956, the UF's program was placed under NCAA sanctions, this time a two-year probation for illegal transportation of athletes from the Northeast.

The vital signs were not the greatest until the revival came in 1990 with the hiring of basketball coach Lon Kruger from Kansas State and the bringing home of The Prodigal.

Looking back on those dark days, it would be hard to believe what good fortune could be ahead for Florida.

VIII. 'you didn't hear Rocky Top much'

This was the time for the kid from Johnson City to shine in his old home state. Trouble is, the Tennessee Vols didn't even put up a good fight. You just couldn't get that true feeling of a spirited, let's-get-ready-to-rumble competition as they lined up against each other in September of 1994.

By the time anybody got really excited down on the shimmering new green of Shields-Watkins Field in Neyland Stadium, the game was already over. And the drama had already been played out on this beautiful new surface which had only been planted when the artificial turf had been ripped up following the 1993 season.

Suddenly assistant coaches were exhorting Gator defenders to block the Vols' field goal attempt late in the game. Not a field goal that would win it. Not a field goal that would tie it. Merely a field goal that would put some points on the board for Tennessee and spare the Vols the embarrassment of a shutout.

The kicker missed. But Florida gave the ball back on a Danny Wuerffel interception and Tennessee was driving toward the checkered end zone.

'The shutout was preserved and a building block was put in place.'

Arriving almost out of breath on the sideline from the press box, defensive coordinator Bob Pruett looked like a man who wanted to be in the middle of the action. It was fourth down inside Florida's 10.

Pruett called an all-out blitz. The Vols' quarterback was sacked. The shutout was preserved and a building block was put in place.

Spurrier later said he was sorry for almost costing Pruett his first goose egg of the year.

You know your team has arrived when you start worrying about defensive shutouts.

For the most part, the Florida coach tried to remain understated and poised as he sat behind a folding table in a small 15x15 paneled room underneath Neyland Stadium which was so hot it felt like a sauna bath.

However, you could see Spurrier was beaming inside. He'd beaten Tennessee in his home state and some of the media kept probing him about it as if he'd come up with a cure for some dreaded pox.

"Don't forget that I came up here with a Duke team in 1988 and we won," he said, rubbing it in on Vols fans a bit.

"I've been up here five times and we've won three. That's better than most, isn't it?"

And amusing himself, Spurrier noted of the Tennessee band: "I didn't hear Rocky Top being played all that much tonight."

It was a little dig, of course, since Vol fans hadn't had much to cheer about. Two years ago they'd reveled in countless versions of "Rocky Top" as Tennessee ran roughshod, 31-14.

As reflected on past trips, however, Spurrier got a little remorseful when he thought about his quarterback. "Poor old Shane Matthews got beaten to a pulp," he said of the three-time All-SEC quarterback.

"It was my fault. I fooled myself into thinking our left tackle could block them and he couldn't."

A measure of redemption for Shane had been extracted on the Vols. Indeed, Rocky Top had not been played much this time on the banks of the Tennessee River.

The 31-0 victory also helped punch holes in this bogus stat about Spurrier's Gator teams being 0-7 on the road against ranked teams. It had begun to surface, thanks primarily to ESPN, the inference being that Spurrier's 1994 team might choke against the Vols, who were ranked midway in the second 10 of the polls.

Instead, Florida prevailed and quarterback Terry Dean held his own personal coming out party, the most accurate passing night of his career, but not his statistical best: Just 303 yards for two touchdowns. His defensive reads were brilliant and timing patterns precision-like.

On one throw to Chris Doering, who curled around the Vols' defensive back and caught the ball just inches from the defender's face, the pass seemed as if it were guided by a homing device.

Suddenly Dean's name could be penciled in on the Heisman Trophy's candidates list.

We talked a little bit about the "Zen of quarterbacking" and how Terry Bradshaw had once been so "zoned out" in a Super Bowl game that he was "in complete control."

Dean said he had felt similar to that against Tennessee on this night. And the way he played in the first half, you tended to believe him.

"I'm finally starting to see the things coach (Spurrier) has been telling me about," said Dean.

It didn't feel so good for Phil Fullmer, nor for those who brought up that bogus 0-7 stat as the Gators rolled up a 24-0 halftime lead and coasted home for SEC win No. 2.

Spurrier said of the bogus stat after the win: "I've thought about that. And if God had told me I could either be 7-0 on the road against ranked teams or finish first in the SEC three out of my first four years, then I'd rather be 0-7 on the road against ranked teams and win the SEC."

What a visitor remembered most of all that night was the smile on the face of defensive coordinator Pruett. Earlier in the day, Pruett had come over to the breakfast table of Jacksonville radio talk show host David Lamm of WNZS and fretted about what might be ahead that night, clearly expressing concern about his secondary. Pruett had once told Lamm: "I'm the 'B' coach. 'B' good or 'B' gone."

That night the "B" coach got an "A."

When you're defensive coordinator for teams like Wake Forest, Tulane and Marshall, you rarely get the chance to coach athletes like the Gators have on defense, particularly 6-6, 271-pound defensive end Kevin Carter and 6-3, 283-pound tackle Ellis Johnson, two phenomenal physical specimens.

Pruett joked about the time in 1993 when he was coaching at Tulane and the Gators were working out at Tulane for their Sugar Bowl game against West Virginia.

"I would press my nose up against the glass, stick out my tongue and drool," he said about watching the Gator athletes enviously.

There were still aftershocks to come. Fullmer called Florida "the most talented team in the SEC." That comment didn't set well with Spurrier, who apparently considered it a slight of his coaching staff's ability.

Spurrier wearies of hearing alumni criticize him for allowing Florida State and other schools to steal so much blue chip talent from the state, and then resents coaches who want to say the Gators beat them with better material.

A few nights later at a Gator Club meeting in Jacksonville, the Florida coach shot back. Spurrier remarked that it was Fullmer who had bragged about signing up such a great recruiting class at Tennessee, including the much-coveted Peyton Manning, son of Archie Manning. Clearly he resented the inference that he had beaten Tennessee because of his better athletes.

When he got home and thought better of it, Spurrier wrote Fullmer a letter of apology and said he hoped he had learned to "keep my big mouth shut." Most thought he hadn't.

By now, four games deep into The Dream Season, it was becoming painfully evident to all, including Athletic Director Jeremy Foley, and gun-shy alumni that Florida's head coach was a headline-maker in more ways than one.

When challenged, The Intrepid One never backed off either in the field or in the press.

The next day after seeing his remark had made big headlines in the *Florida Times-Union*, Spurrier telephoned beat writer John Oesher and said, "well, you got me."

"He never tried to deny saying it," said Oesher. "He just wasn't very happy about the headline. And he wondered why we had to write that kind of story. I tried to explain to him that there were four other members of the media there and we had no choice."

That's the kind of reciprocity that gets Spurrier good will with many writers. He often gets criticized for having the fastest tongue in the South, or for being impetuous, but the large majority of the media feels he is "good copy" and appreciates his willingness to speak frankly.

He seldom lapses into coachspeak, defies many of the stereotypes, tries to score as often as he can no matter where he is on the field or on the clock, communicates candidly with alumni and media and usually wins.

Many alumni and fans--and at least two leading sports columnists in the state--seem to feel that Spurrier should be a little more circumspect before making his comments and a little less provocative in his choice of words. This turned out to be a season, however, in which a couple of Spurrier's players would speak their mind to the media, too.

The last thing the Gators needed as they went on the red clay road to play Ole Miss in their third Southeastern Conference game of the year was another headline of the wrong variety. Spurrier didn't have to worry about that department. Because as it would turn out, his star player, Jack Jackson, would be taking care of the headlines this week.

IX. going one-on-one against racism

Wending your way by car through the Great Plains states from the Rockies to the Deep South, you can quickly tell when you've reached the heartland of rural America.

If baseball is the national past-time up North, then college football is the religion in Dixie.

I love college football in the South.

Along about Oklahoma, the newspapers and the radio get heavy into football. Friday nights you can pick up another high school game every 50 miles on your car radio and when you're not listening to that, you've latched on to some sports talk show out of Dallas or Memphis or somewhere.

Great football players are as revered as great statesmen. Coming in on the interstate to Henryetta, Oklahoma, you can't help but notice the sign that proudly proclaims: "Home of Dallas Cowboys quarterback Troy Aikman," beaming with the same pride of the sign in Little Rock which proclaims: "Hot Springs. Home town of President Bill Clinton."

Pro Bowl quarterbacks and presidents are equally admired in Oklahoma.

'Southern-born and -raised announcers are masters of hyperbole.'

Rolling across Arkansas and into Memphis on Interstate 55, you can see such choice billboards as (my favorites):

"Teeth In Just One Day."

And:

"Cable TV For Your Truck."

Redneck America was ubiquitous. Pickup trucks with gun racks and rebel flags to remind you of Merle Haggard's classic spoof: "Okie from Muskogee." Plenty of country & western music. In this part of America, you can pick up the Grand Ol' Opry on the clear channel station, WSM in Nashville.

Or if you're spinning your dial on a Saturday night, chances are you'll pull in a SEC game from Athens or Baton Rouge or Tuscaloosa--one of those great bastions of Southern football.

Games broadcast on the radio are laced with homespun delicacies and pure pork homerism, but they ooze with charm and passion.

Southern-born and -raised announcers are masters of hyperbole. Nobody does it better than Georgia announcer Larry Munson, the last of a breed, who laments the fate of his beloved Bulldogs thusly: *"There's a pass over the middle and they say THEY'VE got it! But we say WE'VE got it! Our man is on the ground with the ball, but the officials say we didn't get it! Their man did!"*

"Colorful and traditional" would be one way of describing college football in Dixie. Jack Jackson had a different view.

Steve Spurrier had his homecoming. Now Jack Jackson was having his.

In many ways, Spurrier's star wide receiver had adopted his head coach's outspoken nature.

Maybe that's why Spurrier didn't try to muzzle Jackson from saying anything critical about the "racist" heritage of Ole Miss during the week before the game. "We don't muzzle our players," Spurrier likes to say.

Jackson had warned his head coach that if he didn't want him to express his strong feelings on the apartheid that existed in Oxford, then maybe he should be precluded from all the pre-game interviews during Ole Miss week. Spurrier declined to take Jackson up on it, so the feelings came out.

"Coach Spurrier never came to me and said I had to 'be quiet,' because there was nothing wrong with what I said, I was just telling the truth. They gave me the opportunity to speak my mind," said Jackson.

A reporter asked Spurrier if perhaps he and Jackson were alike.

"Nah," Spurrier said with a twinkle in his eye. "I'm not nearly as fast as Jack."

Later on in the season when Jackson spoke out about being benched (aiming his barbs at his coach), however, Spurrier became furious and called Jackson on the carpet.

Oddly enough, very little about the Jackson-Spurrier rift made the newspapers, while Jackson's pre-game comments about Ole Miss were plastered everywhere, including the Rebs' locker room. An interview with Jackson after a game in which he was benched infuriated Spurrier and the writer was going to take the brunt of it.

As for the racism charge, you couldn't find fault with a young man of African-American heritage. Jackson talked it, walked it, lived it and stood up to all the criticism for speaking out against it.

As a native son of the state where the confederate flag symbolizes all that he feels is wrong about the place where he grew up, Jackson is a member of a Mississippi family which felt the frustration of color barriers.

Spurrier had stated Jackson had a right to say what he felt was on his mind. So the flashy junior receiver with the burning speed and the burning desire left Mississippi was burning in more ways than one.

Jackson said he was offended by the confederate flag's prevalence around Oxford, even though the school officially had dropped it as a symbol. He said he didn't understand why some people had to hold on to the past when the past was so "negative" to so many others, especially blacks.

Spurrier defended his player, saying he wasn't mad about Jackson's quotes. "Jack is a fine young man. Jack's a team player.

"We have absolutely no problem with Jack. We don't worry about his quotes getting the opponent riled up. He was just expressing his opinion about the flag.

"He wasn't saying anything bad about the players or the coaches or anyone. He was just talking about the rebel flag and so forth. And he was just being honest about it. He didn't say, 'we're going to kill these turkeys. . .'

"I'm not going to try and get into a political issue with him. He's got his feelings and he's entitled to express them. We're not worried about other teams using something and getting mad at us. That's part of the game. . .if they want to take any part of the comment and say 'that helped us beat them,' then that's fine. But you can't sit back and worry about a comment about a flag."

Quite frankly, one doubts if Jack Jackson knew the history of his own football team. And maybe not even Spurrier.

Truth is there is virtually no common thread to their backgrounds.

Spurrier played on an all-white Florida team and it wasn't until he became a member of the Forty Niners that he actually participated against or with blacks.

Thirty-two years prior--just one season before Spurrier signed his Gator scholarship--Ray Graves' team temporarily adopted the confederate flag as its rallying point for a week.

The all-white 1962 Gator team pasted confederate flag decals on its helmets for the Gator Bowl game against Penn State, though hardly anything was made of it at the time.

The Civil Rights movement was in its infancy and most Southern schools were barely integrated, if at all. There were no black football players in the Southeastern Conference, period.

The message, though fairly harmless by the standards of the day, was clear to the Nittany Lion team: You damn Yankees aren't going to cross the Mason-Dixon line without getting a fight from us Rebs. Florida won the game in an upset, 17-7, but there were no victorious cries of "The South Has Risen Again."

It was merely a psychological ploy by a bunch of kids and their coaches trying to win a bowl game as underdogs with virtually no political implications. Today, however, it would be an offensive gesture to almost any African-American.

There is a huge difference, of course, in a one-time adoption of a symbol and making it the school's official emblem.

Sensitivity to racism not being what it is today, nobody said or wrote a word in 1962. Of course, the media was also lily white, too, and maybe that's the reason. I was one of them and I certainly didn't comprehend the political or cultural implication.

This was about the time James Meredith had been denied entry into Mississippi. A few years later civil rights activists, including Medgar Evers, would eventually be murdered in the state.

And this was yet a decade before the Rebels would sign their first African-American players. Change came slowly around the SEC.

In 1962, Florida was still seven years away from signing its first black athlete.

Graves gave two scholarships to blacks in 1969--one of them also named Jackson, Willie Jackson. The other was Leonard George. Before '69 Tennessee coach Doug Dickey had already begun recruiting the black athlete to Knoxville with some success, jump-starting his program into a new era of prosperity.

Bear Bryant, his all-white Crimson Tide having been clobbered by an integrated Southern Cal team, finally saw the light.

In the early sixties, Bryant actually escorted Trojan running back Sam Cunningham over to the Alabama dressing room following a 42-14 blowout loss and introduced him to his white players, saying: "I want you boys to see what a real football player looks like."

The next year Alabama's football team began recruiting blacks. And winning big.

X. why Jack Jackson spurned his roots

When he was a kid growing up in Moss Point, Mississippi, Jack Jackson didn't dream of hauling in long bombs in the red, white and blue of the University of Mississippi.

Jackson always saw himself garbed in the garnet and gold of Florida State or the navy blue of Notre Dame. And when recruiters began sending him letters from Ole Miss, it was all for naught, because Jackson never opened them.

"I received letters, but I never opened or read a single letter. I think I talked to a recruiter there once or twice, but he got the picture pretty fast," Jackson said. "This (Ole Miss) would have never been a consideration. I could never have gone to school where they were waving a rebel flag in my face. I couldn't look my mother in the eye, or my grandfather, or all those people who had to go through all that horrible stuff back then."

Jackson's comments made their way back up the pipeline to the Mississippi media before Saturday's kickoff. His teammates and his coaches respected the personal war that Jack was waging in behalf of his family and heritage.

'The band doesn't play Dixie the way it used to play Dixie. . .'

Fact is, there are many remnants of racism and reminders of the James Meredith era on campus. All one must do is take a stroll through "The Grove," that picturesque courtyard just a block from Vaught-Hemingway Stadium.

Framed by the magnolias and oaks that are so old that they've probably heard every secret from the Civil War to William Faulkner to Archie Manning and beyond, "The Grove" was playing host to "Public Officials Day." So you can imagine the lies that the magnolias were privy to that day.

The place has been an integral part of Ole Miss campus culture for as long as anybody can remember.

For many years the town of Oxford was lacking in restaurants, so "The Grove" was where you ate out of necessity. "The Grove" has always been the favorite hangout spot of tail-gaters on foot (without their cars or motor homes) and the focal point of pre-game hoopla. The Rebel football team takes its traditional pre-game "Walk Through The Grove" with the band playing school favorites.

There is still an air of formality about it, a sort of upscale Southern picnic. Even today, the standard dress code among Ole Miss football fans is way above the norm for the SEC. Most male students wear shirt and tie. Many of the adult men are in sport coats and women wear dresses--all maybe just a shade below their Sunday Best.

Only these days, the band doesn't play *Dixie* the way it used to play *Dixie*. If you listen closely to the politically correct version, you can hear the old Southern standard being played simultaneously with *The Battle Hymn of the Republic* in what appears to represent an amalgam on behalf of equal time. This version of *Dixie* may be considered convoluted, or maybe enhanced, depending on one's political view.

Though many things have changed in The Land of Cotton, it has not always been easy.

Rebel flags are still a point of contention, though no longer officially an Ole Miss symbol.

There weren't necessarily blatant displays of the rebel flag in "The Grove," but upon close examination you could see a few protest T-shirts disapproving of the ban.

Some of the more subtle displays of defiance are found on napkins or linings of the bread basket at the private table settings of fans. Some people, mostly middle-aged, just seemed determined to hang on to these last vestiges of their Southern homeland and alma mater. And perhaps understandably so. Tradition is tradition.

Saturday when Ole Miss is playing at home, if you head South from Memphis on I-55 and turn east on Highway 6 you will see a "Flags for Sale" sign without the word "confederate" mentioned. But a confederate flag hangs closely by and if you are someone like Jack Jackson, you're not going to miss it.

As the Gators' bus pulled into Oxford and rolled past the "Flags For Sale," Jackson and teammate Ike Hilliard "just shook our heads in disbelief," said Jackson. Having already made his statement about the racist aspect of the flag, Jackson knew he had to stand up to the test of playing at Vaught-Hemingway, but said he felt no extra pressure.

Somebody asked Jackson if he was aware the rebel flag was now banned by Ole Miss officials.

"Banned? I couldn't tell," Jackson responded after the game, which the Gators won 38-14.

"I saw rebel flags in the stands. I saw rebel flags as we came in. I don't know if that's just a ban they have to save face. But they're not enforcing that, because I see rebel flags all over the stadium. Then why would they ban it?"

In the Florida team meeting, his teammates and coaches joked about staying away from Jack because "you have a hit out on you."

During warmups at Vaught-Hemingway Stadium, several Ole Miss players passed by Jackson and told him that "you ran your mouth too much and you're going to pay for it."

Florida went ahead 14-0 before the Rebels fans had time to fold up their tablecloths and napkins in "The Grove."

In two minutes and three seconds the Gators scored twice, once on a pass from Terry Dean to Jackson and 63 seconds later on a blocked punt.

To the contrary, Jackson went out and made them pay. Even though the Gators played their sloppiest game of the year to date, Jackson acquitted himself nicely, catching six passes, five in the first half, two for touchdowns.

Jackson sat the bench most of the second half as he did so often. Jack's 15-yard TD catch right before the half put Florida ahead to stay, 21-14.

Dean padded his touchdown passes with four more, bringing his total to 17 for the year, moving him up in the Heisman race as he logged three full quarters. It was enough to make one ponder the question: How much of this is Terry Dean's execution and how much is he benefiting from the Spurrier system?

On the execution matter, Dean experienced his worse game to date for accuracy: Three interceptions. This was an omen which portended the beginning of the end for Dean.

The key to this game had been the defense, Spurrier said, as Bob Pruett's marauders racked up nine sacks, 2 1/2 of them by defensive end whiz-bang Kevin Carter, who was now becoming the force that many had suspected he might.

The Gator defense held the Rebels to a school-low of 22 yards rushing. Each week, it seemed, Pruett's unit was getting better and his front seven were especially impressive.

Florida won the game handily, but Spurrier wasn't happy with the lack of attention to details. "As a coach you'd like to see things perfect," he said. "We made some mistakes today. And we left some points out there on the field."

Translation: Dean's interceptions kept us from winning bigger. For the first time all year, defenders got into Dean's face. He was rushed hard by Joe Lee Dunn's Ole Miss defense, ranked No. 1 in the country in 1993, and was finally sacked.

In fairness to Spurrier, he took up for his quarterback. "Terry made some beautiful throws of the corner route to Jack Jackson on those touchdowns," said the Florida coach, trying to ease the sting of criticism for the interceptions.

There are dues to be paid in a contact sport and Dean's body reflected those. After the game outside the Gator locker room, Dean was talking to his family, showing his young wife, Robin, the welts on his back where he had taken hard licks. One of the contusions particularly ugly and graphic.

"Who did that to you?" his grandmother asked.

"Just a bunch of big nasty old boys," said Terry's father, Frank, trying to find some humor in the otherwise grotesque sight of the giant red welt on his son's back. Truth be known, Terry was probably more bruised by the three interceptions. And the real pain had not really yet begun for Terry Dean.

Dean had digressed, but despite his rough outing, he now had 17 touchdown passes and still hadn't played a full game.

The day belonged to Jackson, who stood up to the task in front of his mother, Berthany Smith, his family and his friends. The Gators' biggest sign of advancement: A 4-0 record and an ever-improving defense with five straight home games coming up in "The Swamp," starting with the LSU Tigers in seven days.

About the time Spurrier was winding up his career at Florida, a group of about 25 writers on the first-ever Southeastern Conference Skywriters Tour descended upon tiny Oxford, Mississippi.

One of them was my friend Neil Amdur, with whom I was sharing a room on the week-long trip. Neil, now executive sports editor of the *New York Times*, was covering college football for the *Miami Herald.*

Neil was an aggressive reporter. The story Amdur dispatched out of Mississippi that day rocked the Magnolia State, forevermore leaving its imprint. I remember three words in the lead used to describe the Ole Miss program under coach Johnny Vaught: "Age, apathy and apartheid."

The Johnny Vaught era was coming to a close, an era which marked the most successful period of Ole Miss football. Though he had brought SEC championships, national rankings and much glory to the school, Vaught was neither politically correct nor terribly effective anymore.

Diehard Gator fan Whit Palmer Jr. of Ocala reminded me of a story of how we experienced first hand the manner in which Vaught's popularity had begun to decline and his success had spoiled many Ole Miss fans in the mid-sixties.

On a trip to Oxford for a Florida-Ole Miss game, Palmer, myself and my best childhood friend, Ed Monarchik, were riding in a taxi on the way to the stadium, talking football with the driver, who was not enamored with Vaught.

"We asked him," Palmer, said, "why he was so unhappy when the Rebels had lost only one game and that one by a single point. And the driver said, 'it don't matter--a BEAT'S a BEAT!'"

The next year when The Skywriters returned to Oxford, we all joked about being shot out of the sky because of Neil's "age, apathy and apartheid" comment.

Much in the same manner that Jackson's teammates treated him like a leper, we suggested that Neil might want to remain in isolation.

Neil, who is Jewish, had received some nasty mail which he said in a courageous Miami Herald column "was a slur on my heritage." But he never looked back.

We didn't get shot down out of the sky. And Ole Miss was never the same again.

The fact is that the athletic programs at schools like Tennessee, Florida, Auburn and Alabama were all segregated back then. Once they integrated their squads in the early seventies, they began to flourish. Other schools that were slower to follow suit suffered, such as the Ole Miss program.

Now, 30 years later, despite actively recruiting African-American athletes, the University of Mississippi football program has fallen on hard times.

There was going to be more bad news on the horizon for the Rebels, who would be placed on four-year probation by the NCAA, seriously jeopardizing the Ole Miss program. The penalty made the Rebels ineligible for post-season play and drastically cut the number of scholarships.

Sadly, much of the football tradition had eroded, anyway, at Ole Miss. In a league where the mega-stadiums of Florida, Tennessee and others draw full houses upwards of 90,000 and more, Ole Miss football sometimes can't attract a third that many.

Even the allure of the No. 1 Florida Gators couldn't sell out Vaught-Hemingway--the first time an opponent ever brought that kind of ranking to town. Just 38,368 fans showed up and one entire end zone was empty. Almost 50,000 fewer than the Gators drew for lowly New Mexico State!

It's too easy to paint everybody, black or white, with the same brush. Social change brings about changing conditions and changing conditions break traditions of all kinds--good and bad.

The problem with preserving any culture in an archive is contamination: You keep the bad with the good. To do otherwise, you risk throwing out the baby with the bath water.

The eye of Jack Jackson sees injustice on the Ole Miss campus, and justifiably so.

The eye of a white Mississippi graduate might see it as a preservation of family tradition handed down for generations.

And as you walk among the celebrants in "The Grove," a white person might perceive much virtue: Families dining together. Children romping in the grass, throwing Nerf balls. Grandma and granddad soaking up the fall morning sun. Former classmates embracing as they are re-united for the first time in years--sometimes not recognizing each other at first. For the most part, a civilized group of family-oriented folks enjoying social interaction at its finest.

Though Jackson and others probably can't see it, change IS coming to Oxford, Mississippi. That was evident as we left town, driving west on Highway 6, just past the confederate flag stand Jackson and Anthony had held in such great disdain.

Suddenly six young African-American men in an old Cadillac with Mississippi plates pulled up next to a van from Florida just behind us. The one youngster on the passenger side dropped his pants and mooned the white visitors as they sped past the alien vehicles with the out-of-state tags.

All six kids laughed and celebrated this ritual as if it were a rites of passage, an act for which they suffered no recrimination. Not even a honked horn, let alone any threats of physical harm.

Certainly this is no social revolution, but it does represent a change in attitude for some. Things would have no doubt turned out differently for them back in 1966. One couldn't help but wonder if this could be taken as a sign of meager progress to Neil Amdur, or maybe even to Jack Jackson.

XI. the prayer they never wanted to hear again

Now that the Gators were unanimously ranked No. 1 in all the polls again, prosperity was suddenly abounding. For a Florida Gator fan, "prosperity" is a scary word. You can hardly blame them for their paranoia. Many pessimists were keeping that diehard slogan around just in case: "Wait 'Til Next Year. "

That slogan was truly part of a prayer written in the 1912 University of Florida student newspaper, *The Alligator,* which actually plagiarized it from one of its rival Florida schools over in DeLand: “Let us now bow our heads in prayer and join in quoting Stetson’s motto, ‘Wait till next year.’” Probably nobody realized it would become a battle cry for the next 60-plus years.

The absence of Big Game Karma on the Florida campus and the fatalistic approach to each season may have been rooted at the turn of the century.

In 1906 coach Jack Forsythe's Gators were 4-2 and undefeated against state teams when they lost to Rollins in a rematch, 6-0--something that may have been worth Florida referencing prior to the 1995 Sugar Bowl.

'The first step down the road to a lifetime sentence in Heartbreak Hotel.'

Perhaps we can blame Forsythe for helping foster that curse of losing The Big One.

G.E. Pyle took over in 1908 for the next five seasons, as his 1912 team finished 4-2-1 and participated in a "bowl game" of sorts.

According to the book *The Gators*, Pyle was anxious to coach a team made up of such stars as Earle “Dummy” Taylor, Harvey Hester, Louis Tenney, Sam Buie and Hoyle Pounds.

So Pyle agreed to accept an invitation from the Vedado Athletic Club of Havana, Cuba to play two games.

Florida beat the Vedado Athletic Club 28-0 in the Christmas Day game and with five days in between, the American and Cubans enjoyed much holiday merriment.

But a controversy erupted in the game against the Cuban Athletic Club on Dec. 30 when coach Pyle disagreed with the call of an non-English speaking official who had penalized the Gators.

Pyle pulled his team off the field, forfeited the game, was arrested and scheduled for trial, but sneaked out of the country. So much for the post-season.

The official Florida media guide makes no mention of the forfeit of the second game. But the post-season play must have helped Pyle improve his club.

The next year, 1913, the Gators opened with a 144-0 win over Florida Southern. However, they lost the next one to Auburn, 55-0, and Pyle's record wound up at 4-3 in his final season. He was succeeded by Charles McCoy.

The most famous defeat of that era was yet to come, that dreadful 1928 loss to Tennessee, 13-12, which deprived the Gators of immortality. This would be their first step down the road to a lifetime sentence in Heartbreak Hotel.

It wasn't until 1952 that the Gators played in a real post-season game, beating Tulsa, 14-13.

I sat in the stands that day in Jacksonville as a member of the Ocala Junior High team and watched Bob Woodruff's juggernaut in action as his team posted an 8-3 record, his best in a decade of coaching, and wound up ranked 15th in the nation.

All I remember is that Rick Casares could kick extra points so far they looked like they were flying in the clouds over the St. John's River.

Fast forward the calendar up to the 1960s.

The only blight on Ray Graves' otherwise outstanding rookie 1960 season of 9-2 was the 10-0 loss to a fairly good Rice team and the 10-7 loss to Auburn.

Although there would be more seasons of disappointment for Graves, at least he brought badly needed hope to the program.

Graves' 1966 team was on its way to gloryland in Spurrier's senior season, ranked No. 5 in the polls with a slick 7-0 record, when Georgia came to Jacksonville.

The Bulldogs got pressure on Spurrier and picked off his errant passes. The Gators suffered a painful 27-10 licking and watched their dreams of supremacy die at the hand of Vince Dooley's defense.

My most vivid recollection of that game having dinner with my good friend Ed Kensler, offensive coordinator, my normal Friday night routine. Kensler began telling me of his game plan, which he normally did, and clearly the Gators thought they had Georgia's pass rush on Spurrier negated.

He was drawing X's and O's on the table cloth with a felt tip pen, explaining why Spurrier would be untouched. I believed him. I know he believed in it. They just couldn't get the Bulldogs to buy into the scheme.

The last thing Kensler said to me as he stood up was "Bring 'em on, Vince." Dooley did.

One problem: They didn't anticipate that Bulldog tackle Bill Stanfill would become a one-man wrecking crew.

Every time Larry Smith ran out of the backfield for a pass, Stanfill tackled him. Spurrier had a terrible day because he spent most of it on his back.

When sophomore superstar quarterback John Reaves took his 6-0 team to The Loveliest Village on the Plains in 1969 and Auburn set an NCAA record with nine interceptions, it was a re-run of Spurrier's '65 nightmare.

Charley Pell was cursed by the famed Lindsay Scott touchdown which beat him 26-21 in 1980 which pretty much spoiled an otherwise successful 8-4 season.

One of Florida's greatest wins came the next year, in 1984, when the Gators smacked down Georgia, 27-0, in what appeared to be the SEC championship-clinching game. Maybe the best Gator team ever finished 9-1-1 that season. But Pell had been fired by then and the league presidents took away Florida's first SEC title for cheating.

When Galen Hall took over and guided the 1985 Florida team to a No. 1 ranking for one week, along came Georgia again and blew up its national championship plans with a 24-3 whacking. Still, Hall brought more prosperity with back-to-back records of 9-1-1.

When you've had Moby Dick on your line several times and never reeled him into the boat, you can't help but think letting the Big One Get Away is your destiny in life.

What's a Gator to think? Especially when your team is starting to look invincible through your orange and blue-colored glasses? Almost at the halfway point in 1994, to have won four games convincingly without being tested, not having allowed a single point on defense in a second half of play was almost an embarrassment of riches.

The word "dynasty" continued to crop up in private conversations among writers and fans. Quite frankly, it was getting a bit scary to Spurrier, who was starting to show the strain of success.

To date, this was probably the best-looking Gator team anybody had ever seen, with the potential to become one of the truly great college football teams in SEC history.

So much achieved, but so much yet to be proven with four down and seven to go, including unbeaten Auburn and arch enemy Florida State in Tallahassee.

The problem, now, was going to be overconfidence, fostered in some part by the lopsided scores of the first four games and false bravado engendered by the bandwagon-jumping mentality of certain media.

Only cockiness or injuries or instability at the quarterback spot could deny Spurrier's team of imminent glory.

One of the more optimistic members of the media, Pat Dooley of the *Gainesville Sun*, played opportunist early. Dooley flatly predicted in print after four wins that the Gators were going 13-0 and would be national champion.

Considering how well they had played to that point (4-0), Dooley's prediction looked halfway logical, even though there were still seven regular season games, plus a possible SEC title game and a bowl game to play.

Why Dooley chose to declare Florida as national champion at this particular juncture is anybody's guess.

In fairness to Dooley and other visionaries, however, one did get the feeling by week five the Gators' best football had not yet been played.

There was depth at every position. Everybody knew the offense would be the best in the league, but now Bob Pruett's defense was starting to jell.

The real strength of the whole team was the defensive front four.

Led by the improving Kevin Carter and Ellis Johnson, they were starting to make a strong statement and at times were capable of taking over a game.

Pruett's defense was No. 1 in the league. Carter was on his way to become a force that would make him one of the NFL's top draft picks.

And on offense there was ample young talent. Even the freshman tailbacks, Eli Williams and Fred Taylor, were playing like veterans and were apparently turnover-proof.

Frankly, there really were no visible weaknesses, right down to the superb kicking game of punter/kickoff man Shayne Edge and flawless field goal kicking of Judd Davis.

Senior leadership was prevalent on a team blessed with a bountiful contribution from freshmen.

Terry Dean was on fire and his name was now being mentioned first on ESPN and in the national press on Heisman Trophy candidates.

You had the feeling that things were almost going too good for Spurrier. But by now he was showing the anxiety of a guy who just realized he was going to hit the lottery, having just nailed the first four numbers.

Subsequently, Spurrier appeared to withdraw somewhat, talking less in private to even his best of friends in the media, except on the telephone or during normally scheduled interviews.

"He's different this year," said one of the beat reporters who had covered him on a regular basis since he had taken the Florida job.

Meanwhile, Spurrier was warring with two members of the media, Larry Guest of the *Orlando Sentinel* and Dave Hyde of the *Fort Lauderdale Sun-Sentinel* over old scores that had not been settled.

And his players said he was having more and more meetings--one sure sign that the pressure was starting to mount.

Since the first week of play against New Mexico State, Spurrier had displayed more anxiety on the sidelines. Still, the visor was there to be thrown.

To his credit, however, he had not broken out with any inflammatory statement and was trying desperately to invoke self-discipline. And, as always, he remained brutally honest, almost to a fault.

Spurrier had promised to muzzle himself after the misplaced remark about Tennessee's recruiting class and, in fact, had done so. He was downright self-oppressive at times.

Rumors continued to surface about Spurrier becoming the next coach of the Carolina Panthers NFL franchise in Charlotte, partly because of his background in Raleigh-Durham. Sports Illustrated alluded to it again.

There was also the unconfirmed story about one of the owners of the Panthers telling a prominent Gator alumnus:

"We've got Spurrier." There was another about a rumored meeting between Spurrier and the Panthers, but it was denied.

Steve did his best to deflect those rumors for fear they'd become distracting, but one wondered if Spurrier really wanted to eliminate them completely. He just didn't want to address them now.

In late spring of '94, Spurrier signed his new long-term contract through 2000. There was a catch to the new deal, however. Spurrier had an clause in his contract which had not existed before, meaning he could he could get out of it.

The one little-known stipulation was, that if he didn't want to pay the penalty of a buy-out, Spurrier must exercise the out-clause in the month of December so as not to hurt Florida's recruiting. This was a good deterrent to opposing recruiters who spread rumors about coaches leaving.

Yet, where had all the joy gone for Steve Spurrier? He didn't seem happy.

If you could read post-game facial expressions correctly, even his warm, friendly, vivacious wife, Jerri, didn't seem to be enjoying the fruits of this season. From the opening game against New Mexico State until mid-season, Jerri was cautious about her public display of emotion and what she said around certain people.

"I'm OK as long as Steve is OK," she said. "But there has been a awful lot of pressure this year. I'm been talking to Stephanie Goff (wife of Georgia coach Ray Goff) about it. They're really having a tough year."

Such is the untenable position of a coach's spouse in such a high profile job--even one with the engaging personality of a Jerri Spurrier.

Meanwhile, Spurrier's unorthodox style, penchant for speaking out and his enviable success were making him a popular target around the SEC, where he was known for sometimes embarrassing fellow coaches by running up the score on them.

Many of Spurrier's harshest critics hide in the weeds, unwilling to go on the record or be quoted, which is a testimony to the power he has accrued. One writer in Atlanta, Mark Bradley of the *Journal-Constitution*, with obvious Georgia bias, always referred to Spurrier as "the evil genius."

While it may have been written as somewhat of a spoof, the fact was that it's the kind of shot below the belt that takes its toll.

Nobody is totally impervious to those low blows, especially someone as astute about the media as Spurrier. (That's why it would become so gratifying to Spurrier in December when his peers named him SEC Coach of the Year.)

Spurrier's demeanor is often misinterpreted, yet he seemingly doesn't try to change the perception of some people--right or wrong--that he is aloof, insensitive and arrogant.

Many people mistake his competitive nature for disdain of others and his detached approach as indifference.

Critics get offended because they say Spurrier generally puts the blame for defeat on others, that he never admits when he's wrong.

Sometimes his commitment to the fans is held in question.

He doesn't go to many boosters or Gator Club meetings--none during the season.

His feisty spirit is often mistaken for temper tantrums, such as the slamming of the white golf visor to the ground in disgust.

Once, after receiving a 15-yard unsportsmanlike conduct penalty for doing just that, he is supposed to have said to the official: "You'll have to show me that one in the book."

Some say he has meddled too much with the defense in the past and, in some cases, taken most of the best athletes for the side of the ball he coaches--the offense.

Others complain that he keeps his quarterbacks on a short leash, always nagging at them for minor mistakes and making them scapegoats for all the screwups.

Some Spurrier critics say his quarterbacks often have to take the rap for an occasional poor play that he sometimes sends in to them.

Maybe, maybe not. But nobody's perfect.

If Bobby Bowden of Florida State manifests the grand-fatherly image, then Spurrier comes off to his critics as the petulant young prodigy, a little bit mouthy, but pretty much able to back up most of what he says.

Say this for Spurrier:

He never tried to play politician.

You won't get him to apologize for scoring as many points as possible, or complaining about them running it up on him.

He doesn't duck most of the sensitive issues.

Although he doesn't always like what he sees written about himself in the newspaper, he will challenge the writer only when he feels the information is flat wrong or grossly exaggerated. He'll never back down on a quote, or use the "I was misquoted" crutch.

All this, plus he was the head coach of the nation's No. 1 ranked team with his quarterback contending for the Heisman Trophy. What's not to like if you're a writer?

XII. the 'H word' rears its pretty head

In a year when Heisman Trophy candidates were falling from grace faster than Democratic Congressional incumbents, Terry Dean's statistics were getting increasingly difficult to ignore in the first month of college football season.

Dean's Machine was whirring along almost Porsche-like. That, coupled with the Gators' lofty ratings and lopsided victories, made it impossible for the Heisman voters to ignore him. For the first three games Dean had been just about flawless, thrusting himself into serious competition for the most coveted award in football.

With Michigan's Tyrone Wheatley injured and sitting out the early games and the news that Nebraska quarterback Tommy Frazier would miss most of the season with a blood clot behind his knee, Dean shot up the list with people like Colorado running back Rashaan Salaam, Washington running back Napoleon Kaufman and small-college superstar Steve McNair of Alcorn State.

Five weeks into the race, Dean was the leading candidate for the Heisman, according to mid-season straw polls by newspaper sports departments.

'All the Heisman talk was not making Spurrier very happy. . .'

As long as the senior Gator quarterback didn't shoot himself in the foot or suffer a serious injury and Florida kept winning, his chances of becoming the school's second Heisman Trophy winner were very good.

And you couldn't help but notice that touchdown pass No. 4 against Ole Miss had tied Dean with his coach for the fourth position on the Florida all-time list: Both he and Steve Spurrier had thrown 36.

The difference was that Dean still had at least seven regular season games and probably two post-season left to play.

If, in fact, he was still the starting quarterback. And why wouldn't he be?

History was in Dean's favor. If, indeed, he was to win the Heisman, it would mark the third straight year that a quarterback from the state of Florida had achieved the honor, all three of them different schools. And, ironically, neither Gino Torretta of Miami or Charlie Ward of Florida State were playing professional football a year later at that moment (Toretta was picked up later).

Nobody had paid much attention when Dean started the season with seven touchdown passes in the first half against New Mexico State and then added four more against Kentucky. What turned it around for Dean was the impressive first half of throwing against Tennessee and Florida's stint as the No. 1 team in America.

All the Heisman talk was not making Spurrier very happy, because he obviously felt it was a distraction. "We're not interested in Heismans and things like that," Spurrier kept reminding the media. "All that comes with winning."

Curiously, something changed during the second half of the Tennessee game. Somehow Dean would get off-track with his coach and the two of them were never really in concert again.

Despite the perfectionist's approach to the job of quarterbacking, Spurrier couldn't really deny the results by Dean for four weeks. But from that point on, Florida's offense never got any better and Dean's stock began to sink with every interception.

Clearly, however, there would be moments when Spurrier could have used Dean as a backup to Wuerffel in crucial situations. That was not to be. And as the bigger games got closer, both Spurrier and Dean got more tense and, consequently, never got back on the same page again.

Going into the LSU game, one had the sense that Spurrier was considering benching Dean in favor of Danny Wuerffel.

But how do you bench the leading Heisman candidate?

This appeared to be a great spot for an upset by LSU, who by most everybody's judgment was much better than its 1-3 record indicated.

Most of Florida's players and coaches and the media covering the Gators had seen the debacle that Saturday afternoon in Knoxville, just before the Tennessee game. Curly Hallman's team had taken a three-touchdown lead against Auburn, only to see his Tigers self-destruct with three second-half touchdowns on interceptions, which Auburn returned for scores.

LSU should have beaten Auburn--AT AUBURN!--and ruined young Terry Bowden's perfect record, but blew the chance. This turned out to be an ominous message to Spurrier when he got around to playing Auburn: Beware of the interceptions!

Yet the bookmakers didn't respect LSU, because they installed Florida a heavy 27 1/2-point favorite. That's what Spurrier's coaching style does to the gambling community. Bookmakers fear his penchant for burying opponents by huge margins.

In general, the Gator coach seemed to be getting edgier each week. Writers on the beat, his players and friends noticed that he was wearing his so-called "game face" more than usual. The everyday beat writers were considering starting a pool on when Spurrier would explode with another inflammatory remark.

There was also concern about a hangover effect from Ole Miss as the Gator offense came out and staggered. Dean had thrown three interceptions against the Rebels. Even though Florida had never really been in danger of losing, the game was actually tied at 14-14 in the first half.

So was this the first crack in the facade, or just an anomaly? Florida's combustible offense which had produced more points in the first five minutes of the first four games than some teams score in an entire season, wasted no time in rolling up a 14-0 lead on LSU, thanks to Fred Taylor's 16-yard run and a 5-yard TD pass from Dean to Jack Jackson.

The defense padded that to a 20-0 lead on Anthone Lott's 88-yard return of an interception. Then everybody lost interest and the game deteriorated into three hours of unmitigated boredom.

All that depth on the Florida squad soon thinned out as the Gators also lost two key players to injury. Left tackle Jason Odom would be out for four weeks with a knee injury, which meant Florida didn't have its best offensive lineman for the upcoming Auburn game.

And freshman running back Elijah Williams, heretofore the team's leading rusher, suffered a knee and ankle injury that turned out not to be as terrible as it looked, but would still sideline him for a month. He would never return to form.

Coupled with injuries to starting defensive lineman Henry McMillian, reserve freshman tailback Ty Baker and starting linebacker Dexter Daniels, suddenly there was a dent in this talent-laden team at the worst possible time.

That was the bad news. The good news was that Florida won with relative ease, 42-18, over LSU and that Taylor had rushed for 136 yards, putting him ahead of Williams in that statistical category.

"Now he's the tailback," Spurrier said of Taylor. "Somebody asked me the other day, 'are those guys going to alternate for the next four years?' And I said, 'one of them may sprain an ankle and then the other one may have to carry the ball 35 or 40 times a game. . . .' So Fred's it now."

The most disturbing aspect of the LSU game was that the offense stumbled at times. Dean threw three picks and the defense had mental lapses.

This was not very good timing for what lay ahead with two red-letter dates: Oct. 15 at Florida Field against Auburn and Nov. 26 in Tallahassee against Florida State; the best shot a Florida team ever had for a national title; and maybe even another Heisman Trophy winner.

Despite all the Heisman hub-bub, and despite Florida's high ranking and undefeated record, most of the state's attention by the week of the Gators' game against LSU wouldn't be on "The Swamp."

This was also FSU-Miami week. In a state where all three major college teams wind up in the Top 10 or better almost every year, the media finds it impossible to ignore the two of them who HAVE won national championships whenever they play each other. The Hurricanes having lost to Washington--their first defeat at the Orange Bowl in 58 games--took a little luster off, but it would still be ESPN's national game.

Miami would wind up prevailing over Florida State, as Bobby Bowden elected to bench his starting quarterback, Danny Kanell, during the game to no avail. Later, Bowden would learn to regret that decision and come to realize just how bad a mistake he had made benching Kanell.

At a time when neither the Hurricanes or the Seminoles appeared to be set on a quarterback, Spurrier had an embarrassment of riches with Dean, last year's sometimes freshman starter Danny Wuerffel (22 touchdown passes) and big-arm sophomore Eric Kresser all capable of moving the Gator offense.

Dean's Heisman hopes hinged on the Gators' ability to win big games against Auburn and FSU. And his team's No. 1 ranking was beginning to look solid.

Other strong candidates were also beginning to fall along the wayside and there was going to be a clear shot to the Heisman for Florida's quarterback.

With Frazier out for the season, Nebraska's cupcake schedule had now become an albatross for Husker fans, which meant Florida could probably hold serve in the top spot.

Unless the Cornhuskers hammered every opponent, they'd never pass the Gators without Florida losing.

Things were set up for the Gators to run the table.

Yet there was this nagging feeling that Florida's fortunes might be on the downturn instead of the upsurge. And even Spurrier was beginning to appear ruffled.

XIII. 'just say that we played like crap'

Something was wrong with this picture: Florida was unbeaten, ranked No. 1 in the polls, heavily favored at home against unbeaten Auburn. Yet Spurrier was so upset about how his team played against LSU that he asked the press to downplay its potential ability.

In a rare request of the media--although he delivered the "plea" somewhat tongue-in-cheek--Spurrier asked that they write "that we played like crap" after the LSU win. He said he thought that would help his team, his quarterback and the Florida cause.

How often does a coach ask for negative publicity?

The was a cry of desperation here and Spurrier's sixth sense was telling him that the season was starting to slide away from him. Wanting to help out the Gator cause, I went back to my Ocala home and wrote this column, which never actually got published in a newspaper. But I wanted to do my part to help:

OK, I'm in. You can count on me for some of that venomous, negative, hypercritical prose to diss those Florida Gators. And, in case any of you Gator diehards need it, I also have:

'National championships are only to be won by Miami and Florida St.'

The unlisted telephone number for Bandwagon Jumpers Anonymous, Society For The Prevention Of Orange & Blue Dependency, and The Florida Gator Football Fans Trauma Center.

Or, you can just dial 1-800-PESSIMIST.

What Gator fans need to offset this overdose of optimism is a good history lesson, or grievous mistakes will be repeated. Lest you forget: National championships are only to be won by Florida State and Miami in this state. NOT the Florida Gators!

Let's face it: There's just too much joy, happiness and inscrutable bliss abounding in Gator country these days. This stuff has got to cease or we'll be forced to send game films, C.O.D. to your house, of the 1965 Sugar Bowl or the 1968 Georgia Blowout (51-0).

So come off that national championship stuff right now. And start remembering the lessons of your upbringing:

The Gators aren't supposed to be winning like this because their fans don't deserve it. Beat Auburn? Get those impure thoughts out of your head. The Gators are NOT going to beat undefeated Auburn.

Here, let me help you: Auburn 150, Florida 10. Why? Because the Gators are going to "play like crap."

I'm responding to the emergency call of Spurrier, who put out an all-points bulletin for cynics and curmudgeons.

Spurrier suggested that the Florida press corps could help out by being a little more critical. We could all hear his clarion call, loud and clear, after the 42-18 win over LSU: "We're not nearly as good as all you guys think we are. So quit saying we are. That may help us.

"That may help Terry Dean and this whole offense if you guys would say they looked like crap out there today. Maybe that's what we need right there."

He actually said that. Honest.

Hold it, Steve. You just lose the football games. Let us handle the excuses, because I've already got them (with apologies to David Letterman):

Top Ten Reasons Gators' Dynasty Fizzled Vs. LSU And They'll Lose On Saturday

10. Beano Cook and Lee Corso picked them to win.

9. Jeremy Foley. (I just put his name in the book because I promised that I would. It wasn't really his fault.)

8. Spurrier called lousy plays because Terry Dean passed him on all-time touchdown passes list with TD No. 37.

7. Spurrier afraid Dean would win Heisman Trophy.

6. Florida feared its No. 1 ranking would frighten Auburn, Tigers wouldn't show up and fans would demand refund.

5. Writers weren't notified they were supposed to say Gators "look like crap."

4. Gators looked "like crap" because that's what their coach wanted.

3. "Mr. Two Bits," long-time self-appointed cheerleader George Edmondson, missed first game in 10 years with illness.

2. Distracted by Gator Basketball Midnight Madness Friday night and their chorus line with the Dazzlers.

1. It's the curse of them Bowden Boys again!

Of course you realize we were just having a little fun with you Gator fans and none of this stuff was serious.

We really think the Gators will beat Auburn 88-0, win the SEC Championship Game over Alabama, 99-0.

They'll be voted the national college champion and to decide to play in the Super Bowl and kill the Forty Niners.

And then their coach, George Seiffert, will be asking us to write that his team "played like crap."

Dean's lackluster performances the past two weeks were sticking in Spurrier's craw. When asked about it, Spurrier, declining the invitation to criticize his quarterback, said in his post-game LSU press conference: "I'm afraid I'm going to have to use one of those old coaching quotes: 'I've got to wait and see the films.' Except we use tapes now instead of film."

Evidently Spurrier didn't like what he saw on the tapes. Monday when he saw Dean coming out of the elevator, he asked him to come to his office. Dean had no idea he was about to get the worst butt-chewing he'd ever had in five years under Spurrier.

XIV. 'Midnight Madness' was really that

Seldom has the air been more rarefied in Gainesville than it was on the 24th hour of Oct. 14, 1994 which bled over into midnight and became That Fateful Day Of Infamy in Gator football annals, Saturday, Oct. 15.

There was almost a mystical quality to this cloudy, gray Indian summer weekend. Between the Big Football Game and the official opening of basketball on Saturday at 12:01 a.m., the level of excitement on campus was off the charts.

The confluence of the two emotional tides brought a rush of hysteria to the Florida campus unparalleled in school history.

There was a merging of the basketball and football spirits, with Lon Kruger's 1994-95 squad opening practice under the auspices of "Midnight Madness" that seemed so appropriate on the eve of the Florida-Auburn football game.

The "Madness" would extend far beyond midnight, well into the next 16 hours, further intensifying the most important football game ever played at Florida Field.

'I've never seen the atmosphere as charged in my life'--Jeremy Foley

"I've never seen the atmosphere as charged in my life," said Athletic Director Jeremy Foley, who was sitting courtside for the basketball game and in his usual box for the football game the next afternoon.

There won't be many times when both Florida programs are as primed as they were at this juncture in October of 1994: The football team, coming off an SEC championship and victory in the Sugar Bowl, now ranked No. 1 in the nation and playing undefeated Auburn in "The Swamp;" the basketball team about to kick off a new year after making the Final Four for the first time in 75 years of competition.

You could feel the sensory overload everywhere.

There was even a nervous edge to the group of several hundred students milling around the O'Connell Center Friday night, just across from Florida Field, all hoping to eventually get inside and watch "Midnight Madness."

Inside there was already standing room only. The students weren't the only ones shut out. A number of adult fans drove to Gainesville from neighboring cities, couldn't find a parking place and left.

The O'Connell Center was rocking with the anticipation of the raucous, carnival-like introduction of Kruger's basketball team which was being televised live on ESPN. After two hours of Karaoke and a Celebrity Free Throw Shooting Contest won by *Gainesville Sun* Sports Columnist Mike Bianchi, the Gator basketball team made its debut in street clothes for a dance routine with a team of female precision dancers aptly named "The Dazzlers." The crowd roared approval.

When the team showed up the second time, in uniform, at 12:01 for a slam dunk contest, the inflatable roof on the O'Connell Center must have pooched skyward a couple of miles.

Everything about the night and the weekend had that Big Game Feeling and it was as if no structure was big enough to contain the excitement.

Yet there was also a negative undercurrent. So many Gator football fans had been down the Big Game road before. If some of the more experienced ones weren't in denial, then they were overcompensating with a cocksure attitude.

Some of the more arrogant types felt it was their team's inalienable right to punish Terry Bowden for having spoiled an otherwise spotless conference record the year before with a 38-35 Auburn win. Some were also upset that Bowden had inferred the 1993 SEC title game between Florida and Alabama--two teams his Tigers had beaten--represented the Also-Rans Bowl. You could hear a lot of that vindictive stuff on local talk radio.

Even though Auburn was on probation again and wouldn't be able to play in the 1994 SEC title showdown, this game took on the added significance because of national championship possibilities for both teams. Or, at least in the minds of some, but not Spurrier.

Auburn, because of its probationary status, wasn't eligible for anything other than the mythical Associated Press title voted on by media. But, until there is a playoff, aren't they all mythical?

Auburn, blessed with exceptionally good fortune from the football gods, would be trying to become the first Southeastern Conference team ever to beat Spurrier in "The Swamp."

Auburn. The Achilles heel of Florida quarterbacks.

Auburn, the perpetual road-block obstructing the path of Gator greatness.

Auburn, ranked sixth in the Associated Press poll and undefeated in 17 straight games.

Auburn, whose coach was hatched from the genes pool of the hated Florida State Seminoles, the son of FSU coach Bobby Bowden.

The Bowdens, collectively, had lost only once in five tries against Steve Spurrier. Another Bowden! It was enough to raise the hackles of Steve Spurrier, which it did. So Spurrier had a lot of reasons for wanting to beat the Tigers, even rout them.

Aside from the big ABC-TV audience and all the other hoopla, there were personal scores of yesteryear for Spurrier to settle against Auburn and vice-versa. As a junior quarterback at Florida, Spurrier was taken out behind Cliff Hare Stadium (as it was then called) and given a spanking by Auburn. That assault was led by renegade linebacker Bill Cody, himself an Orlando product who picked off several Spurrier passes as Auburn upset Florida, 28-17.

The next year, 1966, Spurrier gained a measure of revenge when he kicked a field goal to defeat the Tigers, 30-27, at Florida Field--a play that was probably his most influential in swaying the electorate for the Heisman Trophy to vote for him over a Purdue quarterback name Bob Griese.

After the 1969 game in which John Reaves threw nine interceptions, Reaves was asked if he thought the chances of winning the Heisman Trophy were dead, he said: "I don't think I'll ever win the Heisman Trophy." He didn't, of course, and no Florida player has before or since Spurrier. But now, Terry Dean could take a commanding lead in the Heisman race with a good day and a win over the Tigers.

So there was some significant history between Florida quarterbacks of potential Heisman candidacy and Auburn's defense.

Later in the week, Spurrier would tell his team in a private meeting that while he didn't really "hate" teams, he came as close as humanly possible to that emotion when sizing up his feelings about the Auburn Tigers.

Spurrier reportedly said he wanted to beat the Tigers as badly as he possibly could. Not just *beat* them, pummel them!

Clearly, this game weighed heavily on the heart and mind of the Gator coaches, as it would be revealed later. It was to become The Magnificent Obsession of Steve Spurrier and many of his followers, who may have begun whiffing the fragrance of the national championship prematurely.

So many people were jumping on the Gator bandwagon by now that it was almost bogging down with celebrants. Without question, The Gospel of the Gators was now carried to every outpost, a fact that would probably enhance recruiting the following January. The Gators were so revered in Las Vegas that the misguided bookmakers had made them a prohibitive 16 1/2-point favorite.

Two undefeated SEC teams and one of them favored by more than two touchdowns!??

Vegas oddsmakers are usually much smarter than that. Was there no sanity left in this world of college football?

Perhaps Spurrier had been correct the week before: Maybe the best thing the media could have done for him and his Florida team was to write that the Gators were "playing like crap." Except that so far, that really wasn't true and nobody was going to believe it.

Although the Gator offense seemed less effective since the second half of the Tennessee game, Spurrier's unit was still among the top three teams in most NCAA offensive statistical categories--except rushing.

This was the biggest weekend in the life of all the Gator players, but none more than Dean, who was two weeks from his 23rd birthday and, himself, in position to reap more glory than he ever dreamed possible in his football life.

It wasn't known by many people then, but even the Heisman's Downtown Athletic Club had figured Dean as the front-runner.

Plans were in the making for a Heisman Trophy Foundation dinner to be held in Jacksonville the following June, honoring Florida's four previous winners: Spurrier, Florida State's Charlie Ward and Miami's Gino Torretta and Vinny Testaverde.

The Heisman Committee felt there was a strong chance it could also be honoring a fifth Heisman winner from Florida: Terry Dean.

But, then, fate can turn on a dime. That was proven by the quirk that had put Dean in a Florida uniform instead of on the other side of the field. All his young life Terry thought he'd someday be playing for Auburn, where his father once attended school, and the team which he had adopted as his favorite since he was in grade school.

Pat Dye, the Auburn coach when Dean was a senior at Collier High School in Naples, had called Terry's father, Frank, and reneged on a promise to invite Terry to the big Alabama-Auburn weekend for top recruits.

"He told me that he didn't think Terry should come up for the Alabama-Auburn weekend because there would be too many other athletes," Frank Dean said with considerable disdain.

"And he said, 'Frank, you can afford to pay Terry's way to Auburn. Why don't you do that and let him walk on?'"

That made Terry's decision to play for the Gators fairly easy. So instead, Dean was now the starting quarterback on the nation's No. 1 team, the Florida Gators, and with 18 touchdown passes in five games, was on track to perhaps being recognized as the greatest college football player in the land. If he was feeling good about himself, little wonder.

Certainly this feeling could help compensate for the devastation Dean had experienced in 1993 when he lost his job to Wuerffel and went into a tailspin--one which had him considering transferring to another program.

Instead, Dean stayed on, won his job back and was named the Most Valuable Player in the SEC Championship game against Alabama.

Instead of strutting with confidence, however, Terry Dean was beginning to feel the heat more than ever now.

Despite his torrid, seven-touchdown first half in the opener against New Mexico State and near flawless game against Kentucky and first half against Tennessee, he was starting to leak oil: The interceptions mounted against Ole Miss and LSU.

After Dean's poor outing against LSU, Spurrier knew he had to change his coaching strategy. Thus he would revert to a hardball role with Dean.

It was not a language that Dean would be able to translate into results on the field.

As a player at Florida, Spurrier was known for his cool, calm, deliberate style. He always had a plan and it seemed to work best when the stakes were highest in the final moments. Despite his tempestuous nature as a coach, visor-flinging and all, Spurrier's teams were always known for their exceptional poise and preparation.

One hallmark of a Spurrier offense was its fast starts out of the blocks which often resulted in scores in the first couple of possessions. The element of surprise, catching the defense off guard early, has always been a powerful weapon in the Spurrier arsenal. Striking quickly against Auburn was imperative.

Over the previous two weeks you could sense the pressure mounting and see the tension building in Spurrier as his quarterback began making more mistakes.

Dean's interceptions against Ole Miss and LSU had unnerved the Gator coach, especially since the senior quarterback had played so well three weeks prior.

And especially since they had talked so much about not making mistakes against undefeated Auburn.

Yet expectations of Terry Dean were never higher. Expectations of Florida football were never higher. The stress impacted everybody.

What was a coach to do? His team was ranked No. 1 in the country, his quarterback was leading the Heisman race and yet there was a problem with the offense which he could only correct through Dean--either by eliminating interceptions or benching him.

If Spurrier had wanted to bash Dean after his three-interception game against LSU, he certainly had the audience and the chance in the post-game press conference. He had resisted.

But now, on a Monday morning after LSU, as Dean stepped off the elevator on his way to see John Reaves, Spurrier summonsed his fifth-year senior quarterback to his office where he would deliver the bad news.

Dean knew the conversation was going to be serious when Spurrier closed the door.

The coach told his quarterback that he had reviewed the tapes of the LSU game and that two of his passes--one to Jack Jackson and another to Aubrey Hill--were so poorly thrown that they had caused him insomnia.

Then, said Dean, Spurrier asked him a curious question: Which sport required the greatest concentration for the longest period of time?

Being a golfer himself and knowing his coach was also an avid player, Dean guessed that it might be the game of golf.

According to Dean, Spurrier said: "I heard Howard Cosell say one time that race car drivers had to concentrate harder than any other athletes. Because they've got to stay focused for three hours behind that wheel. And that's what you've got to do against Auburn."

In and of itself, not a bad analogy. But then came the more harsh reminders in the form of admonition to Dean:

1)To get those absurd thoughts about the Heisman Trophy out of his head which his father, Frank, was alleged to have helped put there;

2)If he continued to make mistakes, like interceptions, he could expect to be yanked from the game.

Spurrier doesn't recall it that way and, in fact, said he wasn't sure which so-called "meeting" to which Dean was referring.

"Before the game I said to him, 'you need to play, now! And you need to concentrate all the way through he game.' And I also told him, 'nobody would love for you to finish the year as our quarterback more than me. I don't want to have to change quarterbacks. I'd love for you to go the whole year. Danny Wuerffel's got two more years.'

"And I said, 'but if you don't run this offense, I'm going to give him a chance. I've got to.' He realized he needed to play better. So if that's too much pressure, then that's too much pressure."

Spurrier at first claimed there was nothing that unusual about the meeting with Dean.

"We just watched the tape. I just got on him the way I got on Jack Jackson, the way I got on Shane Matthews, or anybody else when they don't play as well as they're capable of playing."

Once he reflected on it, however, Spurrier admitted that he did, in fact, "get on him a little more than usual" after the LSU game . "I'm not trying to be critical of him, but he didn't play as well as he should have (vs. LSU)."

No matter what happened in the meeting, it's true that from the very first year on, Dean and Spurrier had clashed.

"I don't know what it was," said a senior teammate and friend of Dean's.

"When they are away from football, playing golf or whatever, they got along OK. But when it came to football--quarterback and coach--there has always been a lot of tension. The two of them just didn't seem to like each other."

Spurrier is known for his strict tutelage of quarterbacks and his lack of patience for same, but few coaches get more out of the position than he does.

To some, it seemed Spurrier criticized Dean excessively, but those who witnessed his confrontations with Shane Matthews from 1990 to 1993 said Spurrier was fair with all his quarterbacks. Spurrier acknowledges that he expected a great deal from his quarterbacks, but that he treated Dean "no differently than I did the others."

This was especially ironic in view of the fact that Dean had been Spurrier's very first player to commit to Florida, just two days after he was named coach.

Even discounting past history, this was an especially unorthodox way to prepare a quarterback for the biggest game of his life.

As much as anything, it was the manner in which Spurrier addressed the issue and the time at which he decided to do it.

There was also the matter that Dean, an intelligent sort with a 3.9 grade average, never had seemed to respond well to the in-your-face technique.

"I've never experienced anything like that," Dean said of the Monday meeting. "My knees were shaking."

His brash nature often confounds the Spurrier faithful, as well as his critics or his own players. Say what you will about Spurrier, but he won't hide behind coaching axioms. He won't tell white lies to a recruit or promise him playing time at a position where he knows there is an abundance of upperclassmen starters.

That conviction perhaps cost Spurrier a chance at signing such hot quarterbacking prospects as Peyton Manning (Tennessee) and Eric Zeier (Georgia). And he doesn't sugar-coat his comments to his quarterbacks, either.

Even by those standards, however, the Spurrier-Dean meeting on the Monday before Auburn which mis-fired was indicative of a troubled time: Coach and a player clashing when they needed to be on the same page. They should have been sidestepping the tension instead of conjuring it up.

If Spurrier hadn't actually meant what he'd said to Dean on Monday or wanted to nullify it, he certain did nothing to dispel those remarks. Because on Friday before the game he again reminded Dean that if he made the kind of mistakes he'd made in recent weeks he would get the hook.

Friday was also the time when Spurrier was drawn into the issue of Auburn's legitimacy as a potential national champion. Asked by ESPN about the title implications of the upcoming game, Spurrier remarked that it would be difficult for the Tigers to be considered a real contender because they weren't eligible to play for the SEC trophy.

Spurrier never worries about the other team using his comments for a bulletin board in the locker room and he had very little concern about Terry Bowden trying to use anything he said to incite his team. He also questioned the toughness of Auburn's schedule.

This is an admirable position and a refreshing outlook by coaches, who are generally so paranoid about the clothes they wear and the food they eat that they become neurotic. He was right, of course, but, again, Spurrier's timing was vulnerable to second-guessing.

"They were trying to find something critical to say about me," Spurrier would charge later.

"He (the ESPN announcer) said, 'do you think Auburn deserves the national championship?'

"Here it is the middle of the year and I said, 'right now I don't think you can put Auburn in the same category with those teams that have been up there year after year--FSU, Miami, Nebraska, etc.'

"I was just trying to be honest. At that point, I just couldn't see Auburn--not even being eligible for the SEC championship game-- (winning a national title) even they went 11-0.

"Do you concede that they would have won both games and give them a national championship? The team that wins the national championship has to win a bowl game on New Year's Day."

ESPN, hoping for a strong retort from Terry Bowden, showed the Auburn coach Spurrier's comments on Saturday. It is estimated that Bowden may have set a new world record in 100-meter dash on his way to his players to tell them about Spurrier's remarks.

XV. something was amiss on the first snap

All week long the pressure of the Auburn game resonated in "The Swamp," gripping the coaches, the players and even the administrative staff of Florida. "Even the secretaries were uptight," said one athletic department employee.

Pressure destroys your routine if you let it--disrupts timing and plants seeds of doubt. Apparently that's what it was doing to the Gators, which was evident when they came out over the ball on the first possession, because clearly something was amiss.

On the first play, Fred Taylor, who would have to play the entire game because of injury to fellow freshman tailback Elijah Williams, was stuffed for no gain. On second and 10 it looked almost like a broken play as Dean took the snap and gained one yard on what appeared to be an unscheduled quarterback sneak.

Center David Swain had snapped the ball on the wrong count. All week long the Gators practiced going on a four-count snap. Instead, Swain snapped the ball on two. Dean was caught off guard. This was not some rookie freshman, but Swain, the senior pre-med major, All-Academic SEC.

'Something was out of sync. That set the tone of the game.'

Suddenly Spurrier's offensive powerhouse, averaging 51 points and 506 total yards per game, looked impotent. Dean's pass was dropped by Reidel Anthony on third down and it didn't matter, because the Gators would have been assessed a 15-yard personal foul penalty anyway, which Auburn declined. Shayne Edge came in to punt.

For one of the few times of the season, it was three-and-out for a Spurrier offense. There was a flag against Florida for illegal procedure, which Auburn declined. Something was out of sync. That set the tone of the game.

On Auburn's first series it became clear that Bob Pruett didn't have the defensive scheme to stop the Tigers

"It was a our worst defensive game of the year," Spurrier would say later. One, by the way, which exposed grave weaknesses in the Gator secondary. But, of course, you could also point to those six turnovers by the offense.

Auburn quarterback Patrick Nix looked worthy of the Downtown Athletic Club's trophy, himself, as he maneuvered his team 68 yards downfield for a quick touchdown, something that Spurrier's team was generally so proficient at doing.

The 32-yard pass from Nix to Thomas Bailey for the touchdown may not have been nearly as disturbing to Florida coaches as the pass that Tiger tight end Andy Fuller caught for 20 yards in that drive. No Gator defender had been within 10 yards of Fuller, a fact that Terry Bowden and his staff did not forget to exploit all afternoon.

There was worse news to come: On the Gators' second series, first play, Swain once again failed to snap the ball on the correct count and there was an even more disastrous result: Dean fumbled and Auburn recovered at the Florida 19. Within minutes Auburn had a field goal and a 10-0 lead with just under six minutes played.

What, pray tell, had happened to this Florida offensive juggernaut?

In the stands, David Peek, a former Gator offensive lineman from Ocala, turned to his brother, Gene, a former Gator receiver, and asked: "*When* are the Gators coming out of the lockerroom?"

Peek was right--the Gators had left their game behind. Auburn wasn't stopping Florida--*Florida* was stopping Florida.

What ensued was a wild afternoon of give and take, with the Gators doing most of the giving and the Tigers most of the taking. Florida would yield six turnovers, yet still have the game in hand until the last 90 seconds.

Terry Dean would disintegrate into oblivion, never to return again to his position of honor as a Gator quarterback. After the shaky start, Dean brought his team back momentarily with a 42-yard touchdown throw to Jack Jackson and even took the Gators to a 14-13 lead midway through the second period.

Spurrier may not have had his best week coaching, but he did have a few good calls left in him. The credit for Jackson's second touchdown--a four-yard run--had to go to the Gators' head coach. On fourth down and one at the Auburn four-yard line, Jackson went in motion toward Dean and just as he passed behind his quarterback, took a handoff, spun away from a tackler and made it into the end zone by sheer force. A brilliant call!

Despite all the problems Florida still led--but not for long. By halftime, Auburn was ahead again, 22-14, and Nix was on his way to a career day. Maybe even a career.

Fuller, in fact, had enjoyed his own career day in the first half alone: The Auburn tight end had caught just two balls all season and already had five in the first two quarters. Gator strong safety Lawrence Wright, whose assignment it was to cover the tight end, just couldn't seem to find him.

Even though he had taken Spurrier's warnings to heart and studied film intently all week, Dean didn't execute his passes.

"Paralysis by (too much) analysis," Dean would say later, referring to his own lack of confidence despite more film study than normal. By the half Dean had already thrown three interceptions, two of them picked off by Auburn free safety Brian Robinson.

Four major contributing factors were:

1)Terrific pressure by the Auburn front four of Willie Whitehead, Mike Pelton, Gary Walker and Alonzo Etheridge;

2)Outstanding anticipation and execution by the Tiger secondary;

3)Dean's lack of composure, staring down his receivers and throwing into coverage;

4)Ability of the Auburn defense to anticipate Florida's play-calling.

When Dean came out and threw pick No. 4--this one pilfered by reserve cornerback Fred Smith--Spurrier had seen enough.

Off the bench came Danny Wuerffel, who had lost the job to Dean the year before during a bad day on a wet Gator Bowl field against Georgia.

The change was a good one, because seemingly with a new quarterback and new "Bandit" formations in which Wuerffel seemed to cut down the Auburn front four's pressure, Florida's offense had new life. On his fourth play of the game, Wuerffel found Aubrey Hill for a 43-yard scoring strike and Auburn's lead was cut to 22-20.

The fourth period would belong to Florida--all but the final three minutes. Wuerffel was splendid in his comeback role and Spurrier looked like the genius most people had been saying that he was, especially after the 65-yard drive for the go-ahead touchdown, capped off by the 28-yard scoring pass to Jackson. It was 33-29, Gators.

Florida's No. 1 ranking and Spurrier's spotless SEC record in "The Swamp" looked intact as Wuerffel brought the Gators out on their own 20 with four minutes to play. Then things came apart in the Three Minutes Of Hell for Gator football fans.

On a first down at the Florida 34 with just under 3:00 left, Wuerffel fell victim to poor clock management. It wasn't so much the five-yard penalty for the delay of game that hurt as it was the stopping of the clock--the clock he was trying to kill. That made it first and 15 at Florida's 29. Now nothing worked.

It kept getting worse, as if the Gators' emotions were frayed.

When Fred Taylor was dropped for a three-yard loss, then gained three on the next play, the clock was stopped by a penalty against Florida which Auburn declined. Time seemed frozen in perpetuity for Gator fans.

This was the defining moment in the Dream Season. From the opening play of the drive, which Wuerffel didn't get off, this would be an ill-fated sequence, one that would loom large in Florida's Day Of Infamy.

The book on Steve Spurrier is that he will throw deep when you least expect it.

"Field position," said David Lamm of *Lamm At Large* on WNZS radio in Jacksonville, "is a term you will never hear Spurrier use."

Spurrier, perhaps due in part to the book by Bo Schembechler that he read stressing the importance of the running game, has developed a penchant for clock-killing in recent years, running the ball in the second half when he's got the game in hand.

But he is still an attacker at heart.

Some of Spurrier's rival coaches know that's his tendency.

Some of them feel that by playing a more conservative game in the waning moments that Spurrier's aggressive style will leave the back door open and give the opponent a chance to win late. But would he subscribe to that theory here, with the Gators needing to kill off just under 90 seconds to preserve the victory?

Surely it would be more prudent to run the ball on third and 15, punt on fourth down and take your chances on stopping Auburn from driving 70 yards, wouldn't it?

Obviously feeling he needed a first down to win the game, Spurrier called a pass, signaling in an "out" route. Wuerffel thought his coach had signaled in a deep post route with the corner route as a bail-out. Thinking he saw freshman receiver Reidel Anthony flashing on the post over the middle, Wuerffel heaved it in that direction. The result would be disastrous. Interception!

"The whole key was getting first downs," said Wuerffel, who wasn't surprised Spurrier had called for a pass.

"As I was getting hit, I just tried to throw it out in front of him and protect him. Which wasn't a good play, because there was another guy over there. I didn't get the same play called that he signaled in. I tried to execute the play I did get called and tried to look off the one safety and throw it over his head, but the right safety just backed straight up from way over there and I guess it went right to him."

When Auburn's Robinson intercepted the Wuerffel pass and returned it 10 yards to the Florida 42, the dreams of long-suffering Gator football fans went to the bottom of "The Swamp," along with all those other Could-A, Should-A, Would-A seasons.

Spurrier came to the defense of his quarterback and the call, saying "it was third down, so that was like a punt." But you didn't get the feeling he had a lot of conviction in that statement and was only trying to take heat off of Wuerffel.

Of the five interceptions, Spurrier would remark caustically: "We kept lobbing them over the middle for them to intercept. They didn't lob any of them over the middle for us to intercept!"

Now the Gators had to pray the defense could hold the Tigers. Even after their sixth turnover, they weren't out of it with under a minute to play.

There was still hope because the Gator defense had held Nix and the Auburn offense to a fourth down and 10 at the Florida 42-yard line with 51 seconds left. As he had been doing all day, Nix executed under the gun, completing a 14-yarder for the first down. Two plays later, the Auburn quarterback found wide receiver Frank Sanders on a crossing route in the end zone for the winning touchdown.

It was a crushing defeat for Spurrier, 36-33, and probably spelled the end to The Dream for a national title.

Furthermore, it was also another loss to another Bowden.

To make matters worse for Spurrier he would learn the next day that he had been playing against both Terry and Bobby.

The Auburn coach told Hubert Mizell of the *St. Petersburg Times* that he had telephoned his father--FSU had an open date that day--and they had discussed some strategy to try against Spurrier.

Terry Bowden sought counsel from his father via cellular at halftime and dad gave him some useful tips.

Mizell got Bobby to admit that he'd given Terry some coaching advice, although he didn't say what it was. Reportedly, however, Dad told Junior to beware of Spurrier throwing deep late in the game. If so, it paid off as Auburn intercepted the Wuerffel pass over the middle.

Bobby said he was sitting home, screaming at the TV.

"I yelled out, 'Terry, don't forget to run our reverse'"--get it, *our* reverse?--"as though he could hear me in Gainesville. But, then, Auburn did run the reverse and wasn't it beautiful?"

Indeed, Sanders scored a 58-yard TD on the reverse.

Few defeats have been as bitter as this one for Gator fans. And none were ever more devastating to Spurrier and his soon-to-be demoted quarterback, Dean. The ensuing interview conducted at Dean's locker would be a subject of much discussion in the morning's papers the next day and his printed comments would provoke his head coach.

What Spurrier could not forgive, evidently, was the fact that Dean told the press about his admonition that if he didn't stop throwing interceptions, Spurrier was going to bench him. Whatever it was, this would create a rift between the quarterback and coach that would never again heal.

Part of me felt for Terry Dean, whose whole life had been programmed around football up until now. His dreams dashed, he knew he'd never again play college football at the level he once did, or maybe in the pros, either.

Perhaps my sympathy was due in part to a similar situation I had experienced in my senior year as the starting quarterback for the Ocala High Wildcats. Unlike Dean, I lost my job *off* the field because I broke a team curfew on the road trip to Bradenton after the first game of the year. Coach Mike Bucha kicked me off along with Richard Barber, Joe Sigmon and Bill Nelson. It was a grievous mistake for which I paid dearly and, to this day, regret having made.

I never again played the game I loved so much. Like Dean, my heart was also broken. The difference was that my dream didn't last as long as Dean's, because I would never have the opportunity to play for the Gators, or anyone else.

I am certain Dean's pain was greater, because expectations were much bigger. Dean broke no rules And he had a career ahead which could be worth millions of dollars.

So here I was, caught up in the compassion for Terry Dean and his family, but also sympathizing with the plight of my friend, Steve Spurrier, who was about to be fried in the press.

One had to also remember that Spurrier suffered maybe his most painful defeat as head coach of the Gators. Spurrier admits he could have done a better job preparing Dean for Auburn, but I also defend a coach's right to bench a player anytime he feels it's in the best interest of the team.

As former UCLA coach John Wooden likes to say, and Spurrier often repeats: "A coach's best ally is the bench."

Truth be known, Spurrier had already waited too long. If he was going to give Dean the hook, he should have done it before or during the LSU game the week before. But is it fair to criticize a coach for sticking with his senior quarterback, even if he does it a bit too long?

Or, is fair to bench your senior quarterback when your team is ranked No. 1 in the nation, undefeated and favored to win over Auburn by 16 1/2 points?

No wonder, then, Spurrier felt the sting of Dean's criticism, real or imagined.

Dean was a quarterback with perhaps more raw physical skill than any he'd ever coached, and yet Spurrier couldn't find his hot buttons.

So how the two of them would interact during pressure situations would be an interesting study in human psychology. And I found myself in the middle, trying to understand both sides.

I had been one of the most zealous advocates in the Florida media for Spurrier's hiring while I was writing a newspaper column for the *Florida Times-Union* in 1989.

I also believed--and still do--Spurrier to be one of the top three coaches in the game.

So my challenge was to try and remain neutral and loyal to my old friend, while still showing that compassion.

I reflected back on the events of the afternoon, wondering exactly how I had gotten in the middle of this dispute.

Several weeks earlier I had been introduced to Frank and Nancy Dean, along with Terry's wife, Robin.

The Deans were at the Marriott Hotel in Memphis on the Friday night before the Florida-Mississippi game with Ben Davis, the father of place-kicker Judd Davis and an old high school acquaintance of mine from Ocala.

Long before the Auburn game, I had planned in this book to tell the story of Florida's season through several different sets of eyes and ears, including a player and his family.

After meeting Frank Dean and having already talked with Terry on several occasions, the Dean family became a natural choice--especially since Terry was such a central figure in the Gators' plot for 1994. I'd made an appointment to visit with Frank and Nancy at their next earliest convenience.

The next earliest convenience for all of us was the night after the Auburn game. The Deans had bought a house in Gainesville for Terry and his wife Robin, which became a family hangout during home game weekends.

"Come on over and we'll put a hamburger on the grill," Frank had said. Following Florida's loss and Terry's demotion, the timing for such a visit wasn't going to be the greatest.

Having telephoned the Dean residence about an hour after the game and getting no answer, I suspected that perhaps the post-game festivities might have been scrubbed.

That, however, was before I knew the Dean family very well and had any clue about their spirit of togetherness. I had been especially impressed that afternoon with how Dean handled his interviews in a most difficult setting around his locker following the loss to Auburn.

After a hamburger with friend Frank Frangie of WNZS radio in Jacksonville, I said goodbye and stopped at a pay phone to advise my regrets to the Deans before I drove back to Ocala.

"Where ARE you?" Nancy Dean said over the phone with a bit of feigned indignation. "We're waiting on you. Get over here right now!"

Here's the dilemma I now faced: How do I bow out gracefully? If I don't take them up on their invitation, it seems like I had been just another fair weather sports writer blowing through town, preying on the Dean's hospitality until I didn't need it anymore--phony and insincere.

I hung up the phone and drove to the subdivision in Northwest Gainesville. An hour later I would be sitting at the kitchen table of Terry Dean with his wife and father in his Gainesville home on the night after the worst day of Terry Dean's college football life.

I felt a bit like an intruder dropping in on the Dean family at a most inopportune moment, only a few hours after the Auburn debacle.

At first I just sat in the living room with Terry, his brother, cousins, grandparents and aunt and uncle while Frank and Robin were out shopping at the hardware store. We watched the Tennessee-Alabama game and made small talk.

It was inevitable, however, that we would talk about the day's events.

As soon as Frank returned, he asked, "you want a Coke?" and we departed to the kitchen.

Frank Dean poured our Cokes. Then he began talking about his disappointments.

It was not the vitriolic comment of a bitter man or the solicitation of sympathy from his visitor, but a father's hope that some new perspective might be gained about this unfortunate incident.

Make no mistake: Frank Dean is no big fan of Steve Spurrier, for obvious reasons. And right now, he was even less, if that was possible.

"Terry," he said, "has played his last football for the University of Florida, I'm sure."

Then, with a bemused look on his face, he added: "What's funny is that by not throwing another pass he'll set a passing efficiency record."

We spoke of the formations Terry had been given in the first half vs. those Wuerffel ran in the second half, looking for a reason that Danny seemed to have more receivers open. We talked about the pre-game preparation and how tense the environment around the team apparently was all week.

Then Terry and Robin came in and sat down, whereupon we made some more small talk.

During that small talk, I learned that Robin was the daughter of an Ocala woman, the former Patsy Milner, a friend and ex-schoolmate of mine and occasional date of my best high school pal, Ed Monarchik. Small talk in a small world, but big revelation.

Mostly, though, this was going to be serious conversation. It was then I learned Terry's version of exactly what had taken place in those two fateful meetings between Spurrier and Dean.

After LSU, Spurrier had backed off criticizing Terry. Clearly, he didn't want this cauldron of coaching controversy to overflow in the press. By Sunday, however, having reviewed the tapes, with Auburn on its way to Gainesville in just six days, the price of poker was about to go up, along with pulse rates.

It was during the Monday meeting before the Auburn game that it became clear just how upset Spurrier really was about Dean's interceptions.

"He told me that two throws I made to Jack (Jackson) and Aubrey (Hill) in the LSU game were so bad that he lost a night's sleep," said Terry.

"Two," said Robin. "Two nights' sleep."

"That's right," said Terry. "Two nights'."

We talked about the two meetings Terry had with Spurrier and there was no doubt that they had significant impact on his psyche.

I could not, for the life of me, see how Terry Dean wouldn't factor in somewhere along the way in the Gators' future. Florida State. The SEC title game. Somewhere.

In subsequent weeks Spurrier would write a letter to Frank Dean. I never asked either of them about the content. Frank Dean said he did not write him back. It was one of several letters the two of then would exchange, perhaps looking for a middle ground that they weren't going to find.

Words and thoughts are often mis-shaped by print, though not always with malice. Without the benefit of knowing which comments were in response to a specific question or hearing the inflection of the person's voice, it's often difficult to discern the exact intent. Whole meanings can be changed.

I don't necessarily think any media intentionally distorted the comments of Dean that afternoon following the Auburn game. But I do feel some wrong impressions were left with readers and that certain writers tried to prompt inflammatory remarks from Dean, who never took the bait.

I have since gone back over the tape of the Dean interview in the locker room after the Auburn loss.

Judge for yourself, as best it can be transmitted from tape recorder to paper.

Notice some of the italicized lines which wound up as key points in some stories and see if you agree this was a classic case of context obsfucation. As the interview unfolds, Dean has been asked if he had received any prior warning about being benched.

Terry had revealed that Spurrier told him twice during the week he would be replaced if he didn't achieve the expected results.

Q. So he told you twice, it's almost like (the rest of the sentence is not discernible on the tape).

A. He's (Spurrier) the head coach, so he does what he wants. That's the way it happened. I can't do anything about it.

Q. How'd that make you feel?

A. I don't know, the way I played...

Q. Did it surprise you?

A. *Yeah, it kind of surprised me, you know.* I don't know, I guess I really shouldn't say too much about it. It was just one of those days. It wasn't meant to be. Last year really taught me...I put my faith in the Lord. I knew that He had a plan for me. I know this is part of His plan for me, too. It doesn't make me like it any better. But it happened and I really can't do anything about it.

Q. Growing up an Auburn fan makes it hurt a little more? That you would have this kind of day against this team?

A. I guess I wanted this game more than others. I'm kind of numb to it right now. . .in a couple of days I'll start thinking more in depth about it.

Q. You said last year to go out there and not play was the worst day of your life. Does this supplant that now?

A. I don't know. Not really. I guess last year I didn't have a handle on it. *It sucked, I'm not going to tell you it didn't.* But at the same time, it's not the end of my life and I've got other things to do.

Q. Terry, was it bad plays, bad reads, or a combination?

A. The first interception I threw there really wasn't much I could do. I made my read, I threw it where I was supposed to. The first one I didn't even see. I got hit and the guy made a great play, I guess. The second one, coach said drop back and throw it deep and they were just kind of sitting there. The third one was a bad one. And the fourth one was exactly where I'm supposed to throw and the nickleback turned at the last second and broke into it. That's football. That's the way it goes.

Q. Do you worry about if you don't play, Danny is going to be the quarterback?

A. I'm sure. That's coach's decision. *I wouldn't expect any other thing.* I'll sit on the bench like I did last year and wait for my turn if it comes up again.

Q. Terry, I know you were upset to be taken out of the game. But watching from the press box after Wuerffel threw the first touchdown pass, everybody seemed to be jumping and reacting except you. Your thoughts at that point?

A. I don't know. I just kind of withdrew and really just kind of lost track what was happening on the field. *I can't worry about it.* You know. I'm disappointed because my team lost. *It just doesn't seem fair. You play here for five years. All those pounds of weights I've lifted and all those miles I've run. And then something like this happens.* But, again, this is not the most important thing. It happens. You've just got to deal with it.

Q. Did coach Spurrier say anything at halftime? He wouldn't tell us. Can you tell us if he discussed anything else--anymore interceptions and you'd be out?

A. Well, *he told me Monday and he told me yesterday that if I played bad, he was going to pull me.*

Q. Well, I heard that, but I didn't want to write it. I didn't believe it. But he really said that?

A. Yeah.

Q. Terry, what did he say when he pulled you out?

A. He didn't say. He just told me he was putting Wuerffel in. I said, "all right." I knew he was going to. He told me he was going to and he did. I expected it at that point.

Q. Have you given much thought to all the attention you've gotten for the Heisman Trophy?

A. No. *It's hard to worry about the Heisman when he tells you if you don't play good he's going to bench you.*

So that helped deal right away with the Heisman stuff. You know, I never got caught up in that. Never worried about it.

Q. What was it like in the second half, Terry? It had to be tough standing there, like deja vu again.

A. Like the same thing all over again (as last year). It seemed like the second half lasted about 10 hours.

Q. During the week, since he said he might pull you, did he change the routine with the number of snaps you were taking?

A. He did a little bit more. But I really prepared hard for this game, more than I ever have. I watched so much film it was probably "paralysis through analysis." It just wasn't meant to be, I guess.

Q. Talk about their swarming coverage that they put on receivers and sort of force those interceptions.

A. Yeah, they take a lot of chances on defense. They break on the ball real well. They watch what I do real well. I think they had us scouted real well and knew what we were going to do. They seemed to be right there right at the last second a lot.

Q. If you had to evaluate yourself, were you forced to throw the ball in places you wouldn't have because you're not used to playing from behind?

A. Not really. We throw a lot, no matter what the score is. Right there at the end of the half we wanted to go deep and tried to get a quick score and I threw that deep interception.

We had about a minute on the clock and I was trying to force it deep again and it got picked off there. Really, I was just trying to go deep too early, probably.

Did that sound like a malcontent quarterback trying to blame his coach for his own failures?

Although it might be true that Terry Dean benefited from Spurrier's system and may have been playing over his head for the first three games of the season, you wouldn't necessarily see it that way if you were his father.

Try to put yourself in Frank Dean's place: Your son has become one of the premiere college football players in the land, bouncing back from near demise the year before. He's driving a juggernaut, a potential national championship football team with a chance to ensure his and his team's place in history by beating an undefeated Auburn, where you once went to school.

Pro scouts and agents are calling you. Would you have high expectations?

Tonight Frank and Terry Dean were Humpty Dumpty, trying to put their dreams together again without the help of all the king's horses and all the king's men. It was not going to be an easy dream to mend.

XVI. Georgia was certainly on their minds

Following the loss to Auburn, the Gators only dropped four notches to No. 5. With an open date, they now had two weeks to stew about their lone defeat.

Even though they would be heavy favorites in their next game, they couldn't get too down with Eric Zeier coming to town with the Georgia Bulldogs. If Nix could riddle the Gator secondary, what could the SEC's all-time passer do?

"There are some nervous Gators around here this week," said former coach Dick Jones, security chief at practices.

This was the first time Georgia had played in Gainesville in 63 years, the game having taken a sabbatical from Jacksonville for a home-and-home series while the Gator Bowl was refurbished. And Auburn had proven that Spurrier could finally be beaten by an SEC opponent in "The Swamp."

If there is one characteristic that rings true of Florida football teams since the beginning of time: Resiliency. Almost every time after a painful defeat, the Gators will bounce back big against the next opponent.

'It was a special way to celebrate Spurrier's 100th victory as a coach.'

And bounce they did against the Bulldogs with one of the most lopsided wins in the series history, 52-14.

For whatever reason, Spurrier has owned Ray Goff and Georgia, whom his team would beat for the fifth straight time. In the five years prior to Spurrier's arrival, Florida was 1-4 against Georgia.

This time it was the defense to the rescue and the maligned Gator secondary which had been sliced and diced by Auburn rallied to the cause, shutting down Zeier without a touchdown and intercepting him four times while holding him to 261 yards passing.

So dominant was Bob Pruett's unit that Spurrier gave out a record six game balls to the defense.

It was a special way to celebrate Spurrier's 100th victory as a coach, both college and pro. The Terry Dean controversy, however, would never disappear.

Trying to guess who's where on Steve Spurrier's quarterback depth chart is often about as frustrating as asking Bud Abbott and Lou Costello "Who's On First?"

Spurrier has the consummate "system" for quarterbacks and he coaches them to fit the scheme, which is why they are virtually interchangeable.

Once in his first spring practice at Florida, while he was sifting through five prospects before finding Shane Matthews, Spurrier was asked who he thought would be the All-SEC quarterback the next season.

He responded: "Whoever we decide to put in the starting lineup." He was right. He started Matthews and Shane was SEC Player of the Year.

When Danny Wuerffel moved into the starting role against Georgia in the fall of 1994, the Florida coach refused to say who would back him up.

But it was Dean who mopped up at the end of the game.

All week Spurrier had kept it a mystery to the media. Did that mean Dean was backing up Wuerffel? Not necessarily.

The following week after the win over Georgia, Danny Wuerffel started and sophomore Eric Kresser played most of the way against Southern Mississippi. And, again, Dean mopped up in the final minutes.

When South Carolina came to town for the final home game of the year, Wuerffel was No. 1, with Spurrier hinting he might play fourth-stringer Brian Schottenheimer.

Smart money said Dean would be resurrected for some key role in an important game before the year was out. But it didn't happen in any of the four wins between the loss to Auburn and the pending game with Florida State.

That was a curious decision by Spurrier, inasmuch as he had used Dean in the game late on two occasions, even though Florida easily had the victory in hand each time.

As the Gators clicked off a victory in the home finale for seniors against South Carolina, 48-17, and beat Vanderbilt, 24-7, in Nashville, Dean sat, or stood, on the sideline.

Though Spurrier kept repeating that he had done "a lousy job" of coaching Dean, there were no apparent efforts to rehabilitate him or mend fences with the senior. Yet with Florida at 9-1, about to play Florida State, there really couldn't be any quarterback controversy. Or could there?

The media even debated it among themselves. Many of them--especially the national press--came down on the side of Dean.

"The Dean-Spurrier story took on life of its own," said David Lamm of WNZS.

"You don't challenge Spurrier. He's the kind of guy when we were all kids and somebody issued a dare to put your tongue on the frozen flag pole, Spurrier would put his tongue on that frozen flag pole."

One who did not take Dean's position was Frank Frangie of WNZS and *Florida SportsScene.*

"I like Terry Dean a lot," Frangie said one night. "He's friendly, he's accessible, he's bright. But I am totally convinced to this day that if he hadn't told the press after the Auburn game about Spurrier calling him on the carpet and had just taken one for the team by saying 'it was my fault, I had a lousy day,' he would have been the starting quarterback the next week."

Jack Hairston of *Gator Pipeline* also felt that Dean crossed the line.

"Terry Dean is talented and intelligent," said Hairston, "but in my opinion had made an irrevocable mistake when he criticized Spurrier for 'threatening' him. Spurrier interpreted that as Dean claiming that Spurrier put too much pressure on him. He never again used Dean in a 'pressure' situation.'"

Dean also might have still been the quarterback if Wuerffel, who had beaten him out in 1993 and then lost the job back to him a few games later, hadn' t been waiting in the wings.

Certainly Wuerffel was familiar with the system and had proven himself the year before as a freshman by throwing 22 touchdown passes. "And Danny Wuerffel," Spurrier likes to say, "is just a joy to coach."

What saved face for Spurrier is that he got results and wound up winning another SEC title without Dean. Critics wonder, however, how far this Gator team might have gone had he at least not exiled Dean.

Meanwhile, the criticism of Spurrier's handling of Dean kept up in the national press--from *Sports Illustrated*, the *Los Angeles Times* and the *New York Times*.

The press seemed fascinated as to why Terry Dean had been sentenced to Spurrier's quarterback purgatory.

Just the week before the Auburn game, the *New York Times* article by Charlie Nobles headlined: *"Spurrier Grumbles, Terry Dean Ignores, Florida Just Wins"* stated:

"I coach Terry just like I coached Shane Matthews, all those quarterbacks at Duke, John Reaves at the (Tampa Bay) Bandits," Spurrier said on Sunday. "My track record with quarterbacks is pretty decent. I don't see why I should change the way I coach quarterbacks."

In a story entitled *Steam in the Swamp,* a *Sports Illustrated* article by Christian Stone would say:

"The noose is tightened, slow in the drawing, but hard and unyielding in the end. For 4 1/2 years Florida quarterback Terry Dean had sought assurance that his imperfections would be tolerated, that there was terra firma to be found in Steve Spurrier's Swamp. But as he stood on the sidelines after being pulled from a four-interception performance against Auburn on Oct. 15, Dean finally understood.

'Maybe for the first time since I arrived, I knew exactly where I stood,' says Dean. 'I knew that it was over for me here. . .'

'What hurts isn't the criticism from the people who come to games waiting for me to lose,' says Spurrier. 'What hurts is that people I consider to be fair, including some Gator fans, are upset about the way I'm handling the Terry thing.

'I've done a lousy job of coaching Terry Dean. But I've got a clear conscience that I've coached him the best I can for five years now.'"

Under the headline *"Spurrier's Failure?,"* the *Los Angeles Times* story by Jim Hodges would read:

"Steve Spurrier has been accused of being driven, paranoid, charming, manipulative, successful, impulsive, compulsive and sometimes even repulsive. But never sentimental.

"A sentimentalist would have moved heaven and earth to make sure his first recruit at Florida was successful, returning loyalty for loyalty, rewarding effort with praise.

"Or maybe Spurrier did. Or maybe, as Terry Dean said, Spurrier didn't.

"This much is known. On Jan. 2, 1990, three days after he was hired to coach his alma mater, Spurrier and Frank and Nancy Dean lifted their glasses in Naples, Fla. to toast the newest Gator marriage.

"Steve Spurrier, coach, had gotten the Dean's son, quarterback Terry, to say 'I do' to an offer to play in Gainesville.

"Al and Peg Bundy have gotten along better since."

There were many other articles, including one in the *St. Petersburg Times* by John Romano, which dealt with charges by the Deans that since the four-interception Auburn game, Terry had been ostracized by Spurrier in these ways:

1)Wasn't included in quarterback meetings;

2)Was asked to turn in his game plan prior to the Georgia game;

3)Didn't have a roommate on the overnight trips after always sharing a room with safety Michael Gilmore.

Spurrier refuted those charges, saying he was never involved in the choices of roommates, that Terry was never excluded from quarterback meetings and that it was standard procedure to pick up game plans early in the week (although Wuerffel's wasn't that week).

The most revealing part of the story was that Dean would be writing his own book after keeping a detailed journal of tape recordings and that there may be "some pretty hot stuff" in it. In the same paragraph, Dean admitted that he "might be better off just to burn that stuff."

At this writing, the fate of that book was still undetermined.

This was more than the classic coach/quarterback confrontation, it was "war." And it ran deep. In the Romano article, Spurrier did finally acknowledge that he couldn't "win any battle with Terry Dean" and that he was willing to accept wearing the black hat as "the bad guy."

Dean, on the other hand, was still befuddled, apparently not able to understand he had breached the loyalty between himself and his coach. It never seemed to dawn on him that there was more to the ordeal than the interceptions.

Said Dean: "That's really the only problem I've had with the whole thing: I don't understand what I've done wrong.

"I saw (Georgia's) Eric Zeier throw four interceptions against us and nobody batted an eye about whether he should get benched."

At the same time, Ray Goff didn't exactly have a Danny Wuerffel playing behind Zeier, either.

Apparently, as Frangie, Lamm and Hairston had suggested, Dean's sin was revealing to the media that Spurrier had forewarned him about throwing interceptions in two meetings prior to the Auburn game. And, as Lamm said, it took on a life of its own.

Not a very pleasant life for either the coach or the quarterback. And at the University of Florida, where football is played under a microscope, the last thing the head coach needs is a nasty quarterback controversy played out on a national stage.

There's already plenty of heat to go around without it.

XVII. the hottest coaching chair in America

If Lou Holtz thinks the pressure at Notre Dame is unbearable, then maybe he should have taken the job back in the late seventies when it was rumored he was going to be the replacement for Doug Dickey.

While the job of coaching football at Florida might very well be among the top five in America, it is also a bonafide pressure cooker. One reason is the intense media scrutiny.

There are fewer "homer" writers in Florida because of the diverse nature of its population, division of fan loyalty among three successful college programs and a highly competitive brand of newspapering.

Take a look sometimes at the newspaper racks on the Florida campus, lined up in front of restaurants. There are as many as 10 state papers, all of which contain news about Gator football on a regular basis.

Pressure can be found at any level of coaching in any geographical location, but the manifestation of that pressure is not nearly so analyzed and amplified as it is among Florida newspapers.

'You cannot escape the press at the University of Florida.'

The Gators have the country's largest contingent of media traveling with them on the road--regularly numbering in the mid-teens--and one of the nation's largest when they play at home. Daily practices are usually covered by a dozen or more correspondents or staffers. By contrast, a big-time program like UCLA has one reporter covering practice.

You cannot escape the press at the University of Florida.

The job of any Division I college coach comes with major stress. But the job of Florida football coach has always seemed to draw a little more fire than most, due in part to the incestuous nature of politics and sport in the Sunshine State.

It is said that some governors ran on secret back-room political agendas, promising to deliver a coach to Gainesville who could bring glory and honor to the Gators. There is no doubt that the Gator football coach is under the gun.

There is also the matter of Florida's "Sunshine Law," which requires all elected politicians and state institutions to make public any documents or minutes from meetings which involved their business. This was an especially damaging tool which the media used to spade out information pertaining to Florida's NCAA investigations.

Often, Associate Athletic Director Norm Carlson is MVP for the Gators just by the sheer volume and intensity of the controversy he must juggle.

In the end, however, it's probably not so much the media pressure that weighs on Spurrier. It's the pressure he puts on himself.

Amazingly, even with the highest standards ever achieved in Florida football, Spurrier finds himself at the center of the storm. He must lay awake, wondering if he hasn't created his own monster, one he will never be able to satisfy.

Just winning isn't enough. In today's Poll Bowl race, you've got to win big.

It's similar at many other Division I schools, like Notre Dame. The Irish attract their share of national attention, including their "very own network" (all home games telecast on NBC). However, newspapers and TV stations in and around Indiana don't compete as aggressively for news as those within a 150-mile radius of Gainesville.

At Florida, it's all on top of you.

From the outset, the Spurrier family knew it was going to be different than Durham. In the spring of 1990, only a few weeks after Spurrier was hired by Florida, I had an occasion to dine out with Steve and his wife Jerri.

Whatever Steve accomplishes as a football coach will be due in part to how much he listens to the advice of Jerri.

She is his compass, his rudder, his beacon of light, his No. 1 fan, his best friend. She is also his extra set of eyes and ears which often prove to be valuable filters to the outside world. But she also doesn't mind telling him when he's wrong.

They were still in transition from the Durham-to-Gainesville move back in the spring of 1990, in the process of building a house and trying to get their bearings. So naturally, they were a bit unsettled.

All day and at dinner, I noticed Steve seemed to be on edge, and his impatience seemed to annoy Jerri.

Finally, near the end of the meal, I felt compelled to say something: "You two are lucky people. You've achieved a dream. You're back home and Steve has the job he has always wanted. Why don't you just relax and learn to enjoy it. . whether it lasts one year, five years, 10 years or a lifetime?"

There was ensuing silence and I wondered if maybe I had mis-spoken or intruded on the Spurrier family business.

Two weeks later I received a handwritten thank you note from Jerri, saying: "Thank you for what you said."

Coaches today are under siege because athletics are expected to generate so much money and, subsequently, athletes have been granted so much power.

In today's world of conflict between coach and athlete, Spurrier's willingness to take swift and decisive measures in meting out punishment is downright admirable and refreshing.

There has never been as big an emphasis on winning as there is today. I asked Spurrier about all that pressure. He told a story about a friend of his-- a former player at Georgia--now coaching at a small college who was feeling overwhelmed. The friend called Spurrier one day to commiserate.

"And I said to him, 'if you think you've got pressure at a small school, what do you think it's like for me at Florida,'" Spurrier remarked.

To which the friend countered: "The big difference is that when you go to the bank and deposit your check every week, that pressure on you eases up quite a bit."

Spurrier makes in excess of $700,000 a year.

The price of everything has gone up.

When Spurrier was done with his normal Tuesday press conference on Nov. 8, 1994, he made a strange request: "You people in the media, hang around for a little while if you will. I'll be back in about 10 minutes and I want to talk with you."

About 20 media were in attendance. Clearly, something big was going to happen.

"He's going to the Tampa Bay Bucs," Jack Hairston of *Gator Pipeline* said in jest.

Instead, Spurrier was going to address the group about what he felt was unfair coverage of him and his team.

In one of the most bizarre scenes anybody covering Florida football for the past five years had witnessed, Spurrier scolded the group of sports writers--one in particular--whose regular assignment was covering the Gators.

First, Spurrier asked that all the media bring their tape recorders to the front table. The media complied. "Now turn 'em off," said the head coach.

He then asked that his remarks remain private and unpublished, which for the most part, the media has honored. (That subject matter will remain "off the record" here as well.)

What ensued was an emotional plea in which Spurrier never lost his temper, but was visibly shaken.

Long-time observers watching Spurrier pace the floor nervously, choke on his words and tear up as he struggled to hold back his anger, had never seen him so upset.

The reason it was so unusual was that it took place when the Gators were 7-1 and ranked as high as No. 4 in the national polls. Since the Auburn game, the Gators had knocked off Georgia, Southern Mississippi and South Carolina.

They had also locked up another appearance in the SEC championship game with a shot at the Sugar Bowl.

One wondered why someone who appeared so uncomfortable as Spurrier did at the moment would even want a job that made him so unhappy. One also wondered why the best football coach that Florida ever had--and maybe ever will have--would have to use this forum now.

Apparently because of pent up frustrations over the stories criticizing the program and the coach, Spurrier went against the advice of his loyal aide and friend, Norm Carlson, associate athletic director, and addressed this matter.

The last guy you'd expect to succumb to that kind of pressure would be Spurrier, who made his reputation as a Gator quarterback for his grace under fire. The timing was curious.

When your football team is among the nation's top five and on course to wins its third SEC title in four years, you aren't expected to be very unhappy about much.

"I don't know why I got that way," Spurrier would say later. "That happened to me once when I was trying to talk to my team. I just wanted to get some things off my chest."

Frankly, the subject that Spurrier addressed that day wasn't all that crucial, nor that interesting. His body language, however, was quite revealing: Spurrier's perception that things were apparently coming unraveled.

Truth be known, Spurrier had never really been taken apart by the media--and he wasn't being now--because he's always been a winner everywhere he's played or coached.

"A couple of guys in the media were taking shots at me, using my players to criticize me," Spurrier would say. "And I just had it. Like Pat Riley says in his book, sometimes you have to take a stand."

During his reign at Florida, Spurrier has enjoyed an excellent reputation with the media. There is a limit to his personal interaction these days with the writers and broadcasters, although his wife Jerri did invite some longtime media friends to a Florida Field 50th birthday party for Steve. And it was a friendly, convivial evening.

From the outset, Spurrier was warned not to let the media dictate his future when he came to Florida.

"Roy Kramer (SEC Commissioner) told me to be sure and not let the media run my team," he recalled. "And I said, 'don't worry about that. They might run me off, but they're not going to run my team.'"

Fact is, Spurrier enjoys a better relationship with the press than he realizes, better than any Florida coach since Graves, a guy who really worked at it. Even though he won't agree with this, Spurrier has virtually been treated to a honeymoon, with a couple of exceptions.

It has been all-out war with Larry Guest of the *Orlando Sentinel*, whose questions he refused to answer at a Sugar Bowl press conference. Guest says he isn't really sure why the two of them got off to such a bad start.

Their trouble began when Spurrier disagreed with what Guest wrote about a Gator Club meeting in Jacksonville after the mayor had revealed that his city was dropping out of the race for an NFL team. Spurrier, alleged to have applauded the move, asked for a retraction and Guest refused, saying his information was solid. Seemingly so insignificant.

Inside sources said Guest was angered when Spurrier wouldn't consent to an interview in his final days before leaving Duke for Florida. Guest denies any truth in that.

"I went up to Duke twice and wrote a couple of stories," he said. "We were friends back then. It was an entirely different atmosphere up at Duke. When he came here, things changed."

Guest, says Spurrier, has responded by writing what the Gators' coach thinks are out out-right lies and chiding him by referring to him in his column as "Coach Superior." The *Sentinel* columnist claims he has always liked Spurrier and considered him "a terrific coach."

"I said right off the bat that he was better than most coaches on the other side of the field, a 'chess master at warp speed,'" said Guest.

When asked for a written comment about Spurrier for this book, Guest wrote: "Basically a good and admirable person. Peerless offensive mind. Honorable and candid to a fault.

"Exemplary disciplinarian--really a breed apart in that category from most coaches who gloss over player transgressions to keep athletes in uniform."

But, says Guest, Spurrier doesn't take criticism well and is a "self-absorbed" person who "has trouble giving credit to players and coaches." After the differences over the Jacksonville story, "I guess I became persona non grata," said Guest. "He likes to say you are either a 'Gator writer' or a 'non-Gator writer,' and at that point I became a 'non-Gator writer.'"

Attempts by Guest to patch up their differences, he said, have been ignored, even when mutual friends have mediated. Spurrier's favorite comments about that: "I'm not going to kiss any writer's ass." Although it is known that Spurrier is both angry at Guest and some of the things he has written, privately he is uncomfortable about the rift.

At this writing, Guest says he has attempted to arrange for a meeting for the two of them to air their differences, but that Spurrier has declined. Guest says he continues to attempt to telephone the Gator coach to no avail. After talking to friends or relatives of both, I am convinced neither of them were pleased about the consequences of this conflict.

Spurrier being one of the most highly successful college football coaches, this does Guest no good whatsoever. And with Guest being the sports columnist in one of Florida's biggest newspapers, just 110 miles south of Gainesville, it is not the healthiest of public relations situations for Spurrier.

To a lesser degree, Spurrier is warring with Fort Lauderdale Sun-Sentinel columnist David Hyde, who has challenged Florida's decision not to play Miami. Spurrier says it's because of scheduling conflicts caused by the SEC realignment into divisions.

In a poll among those writers and broadcasters covering Florida, Spurrier was lauded as media-friendly and his coming to coach the Gators was labeled "the turning point for Florida football." Privately, many of the writers complain that Spurrier is too sensitive to small matters, but they almost all like him and admire his style.

"I can't imagine many more major coaches in Division I being more accessible," said Chris Harry of the *Tampa Tribune.* "Always returns calls. Will talk off the record. Will treat you as you treat him in regards to fairness. What I like about him best is his frankness."

Yet Harry was one of the reporters Spurrier had targeted earlier for criticism.

Yet Harry was one of the reporters Spurrier had targeted earlier for criticism.

"His relationship with the media is something of a myth," said John Oesher of the *Florida Times-Union.* "People say he doesn't get along with reporters, but those who cover him closely have a good relationship with him."

Dan Hincken of WTLV-TV, Jacksonville: "Offensive genius. Only problem is that he speaks as a Gator sometimes instead of a Gator coach. Bleeds orange and blue through and through."

Peter Kerasotis, *Florida Today,* who broke the "Free Shoes University" story: "It would be easy to say that he has a thin skin and a thick ego. But I really don't believe criticism bothers him unless he perceives it to be unfounded, unwarranted or unfair. I've found him to be very honest and he simply loves to compete. He wants everyone to compete by the same rules. . ."

Hubert Mizell, *St. Petersburg Times*: "A brilliant offensive strategist, an unmatchable asset for the Florida Gators. But a head coach who could spare himself a ton of PR problems by making a pound of adjustments. I like Spurrier. I like dealing with Spurrier. But if I were his brother, I'd advise him to all but stop reacting to media criticism. And, just maybe, it would subside to a major degree."

Mike Bianchi, *Gainesville Sun*: "I like Steve because he says what's on his mind. No mealy-mouth political correctness from Stevie Boy."

Says Frangie: "Terrific play-caller and organizer. . .My biggest rap on him as a coach is that he doesn't stay calm on the sideline. His players, at times, play tense."

Says Hairston: "He's very honest, but, surprisingly, a lot of the media doesn't seem to care for him. Best quality: His honesty. Worst quality: Ultra-sensitive, too thin-skinned."

The blowup at the press conference didn't backfire. Once over, it seemed to clear the air between Spurrier and the print media. And it also seemed to alleviate some pressure on the Gator coach. Except for the Guest and Hyde matters.

On a late summer night circa 1968, in a private room at the Doral County Club in Miami, then-Florida football coach Ray Graves pulled up a chair to participate in a friendly, low-stakes poker game with some members of the Florida Sports Writers Association.

The chair cracked and came apart as Graves, red-faced and startled, braced himself from what most assuredly would have been a painful fall.

One of the writers from Miami, trying to find some humor in the moment that might alleviate Graves' embarrassment, helped Graves up off the floor and then quipped: "You know, Ray, Jackie Gleason actually sat in that very same chair and it held him okay."

To which Graves responded: "Jackie Gleason has never had the pressure on him that I've got on me."

Such is the life of the Florida football coach.

Today, more than 25 years after the Graves chair-cracking metaphor, expectations of the Gators equaling or surpassing the rather lofty standards set by Miami and Florida State have probably quadrupled.

In all the years of covering Graves (10), I never saw him lose his composure once. One reason Graves survived for a decade was his candid nature and openness with the media, along with his ability to adapt and cope with the stress of the job without public outbursts of temper. He was a master politician, something Spurrier refuses to be.

Yet, let the record also show that Graves, despite the most successful one-man decade of coaching in University of Florida history to that date (70-31-4 for a .686 percentage), was pressured into resigning as coach after the 1969 season.

Even though Graves misled the media about his intentions to become a full-time athletic director--the deal was struck prior to the 1969 season--he survived both the backlash and an NCAA investigation over the matter.

How? Graves was always politically correct and knew how to befriend the power brokers.

Graves also enjoyed the best relationship with the media of any coach in modern history. Doug Dickey should have learned from Graves.

Dickey succeeded Graves in 1970 and never fulfilled the promises that he brought to Gainesville:

Namely to deliver the Gators' first SEC title and, hopefully one day, a national championship, which was the goal he set for the program on the first day.

Dickey considered the media a necessary evil and befriended none of them. He didn't want a social relationship with the press. He didn't trust any of them.

Instead of hosting Saturday night media socials at the head coach's house, as Graves had done, Dickey had 7 a.m. Sunday breakfasts which were not well-attended.

Dickey also instituted early morning conference calls that were anything but inspiring to sports writers. In the end, when he couldn't win, Dickey was without any defenders in the media. He was forced out without meeting high expectations.

Dickey not only failed to cultivate the media or play the correct politics, but, like his mentor, Bob Woodruff, also failed to play the right kind of offense.

Inheriting the same basic offensive talent from Graves' 9-1-1 team, which featured a wide open passing game, Dickey converted them into a dull, lethargic group which won just 11 games over the next two years. The 1969 team was loaded with underclass talent, including quarterback phenom John Reaves and fellow sophomore Carlos Alvarez, the All-American wide receiver. But it died on a vine.

Turning this once high-powered offensive machine into Instant Sominex, Dickey failed to win over key alumni and underestimated the clout of Florida's aggressive journalists.

This was not Tennessee, where Vols' practices were usually covered by one Knoxville writer.

"If I kicked six guys off my team at Tennessee," Dickey once admitted, "there was normally only one writer covering practice who would know about it and if we asked him, he'd hold it out for a week before anybody knew."

Dickey forgot what he had learned as a former Gator player: Florida coaches don't do much or say much that's not noticed. The university sits in a triangle of high density population with high-spirited newspapers located in Tampa-St. Petersburg, Orlando and Jacksonville. To them, Gator football is still a year-round story.

Often coaches either try to ignore the media completely or "coach" the media, "coach" being a euphemism for "control."

Some coaches go nuts trying to control everything around them, including their players, the press, the fans and their own destiny.

Charley Pell was one such example.

XVIII. the personal hell of Charley Pell

The fish bowl in Gainesville is quite different than Doug Dickey's Knoxville--different than most other places.

Ask Galen Hall, who never measured up as an attractive media figure: plump and bald with a speech impediment. Oddly, none of that had anything to do with his knowledge of football or coaching skills, which were considerable.

Taking over from Pell, Hall lasted six years--four full seasons and parts of two others--but couldn't survive either the NCAA investigators, his image or his less-than-Hollywood good looks.

After coaching the Gators to 41 wins, Hall was fired five games into the 1989 season after the Gator football program was charged with numerous infractions of NCAA rules, although very little was ever proven.

According to his family, Pell actually helped coach that 1984 team from exile when Hall was named interim.

"Every Monday night and every Thursday night," said Ward Pell, Charley's wife, "the entire Florida football team came to our house to meet with Charley. Charley coached that team."

'It's a miracle I'm alive.'
--Charley Pell

If so, he coached it pretty well. Florida wound up 9-1-1, winning an SEC title which it later had to give back, and was awarded national championship trophies by the New York Times and The Sporting News.

The '84 Gators (voted for this book by a special panel of writers and broadcasters as "The Greatest Gator Team") also finished No. 3 in the Associated Press and USA Today/CNN polls and No. 7 in the UPI Coaches Poll.

But the price paid by both Pell personally and the Florida athletic program wound up being far too costly. Pell is still paying.

Although he will tell you his pressure was self-inflicted, the truth is that Charley Pell had an obsessive/compulsive personality which made him willing to do anything he had to do to keep from failing.

That penchant for wretched excess not only cost him his job, but also prompted Pell to attempt suicide, although he lived to tell about it on ESPN, The Oprah Winfrey Show and Dateline NBC.

Charley Pell is living proof today that football coaches can go temporarily insane and wind up surviving despite themselves.

"It's a miracle that I'm alive," Pell says today. "If nothing else, the way I was burning the candle at both ends, it's a wonder that I didn't blow out a valve in my heart."

At his home in Hidden Hills, an upscale residential area of suburban Jacksonville, Pell agreed one night in the fall of 1994 to share his thoughts on Florida football and his near-death experience.

We sat in the living room and talked for hours about The New Charley and The Old Charley Pell. For me, there was only the "new," because I'd never met him until now.

Why Charley Pell? Key Florida alumni had all told me that without the sweat equity of Charley Pell, Florida's football program would not be anywhere nearly as successful.

One key side note about Pell, the man: Never once did he utter a critical word about Spurrier, athletic director Jeremy Foley or the Florida program.

At first he didn't even appear to harbor bitterness about those who sentenced him into exile after the NCAA investigation, although this surfaced later.

This was a man who just a little over six months prior had driven his car out to a remote spot in Jacksonville after leaving goodbye letters and a suicide note with the wife of a Florida State trooper friend, stuck a hose from the exhaust pipe in his mouth and tried to end it all.

Because the fumes of the carbon monoxide were so strong that they made him nauseated, Charley opened the door so as not to vomit inside his car. Instead, he toppled outside and passed out, which saved his life.

What could possibly cause a man to do this?

Looking back on it now, Pell realizes the major mistakes he made during his regime at Florida, not the least of which was putting far too much emphasis on work in his life.

Among the other downfalls:

■Not keeping better track of the activities of his assistant coaches;

■Dealing with the media in a less-than-inspired manner;

■Hiring one assistant coach at the suggestion of another despite having bad vibes about him initially;

■Taking his "win-at-all-cost" assignment seriously without much regard for the consequences;

■Suffering the blindness of an obsessed man.

And, of course, cheating. Not that Charley didn't bring a lot of it on himself by breaking the rules and looking the other way when members of his staff did the same.

Pell will never say this publicly, but he feels he took the fall for a lot of other people when he was forced to resign in 1984--the administrators included.

It was 10 years before the anger welled up in him and the sense of failure in business and football became so overwhelming that he tried to kill himself.

"I'll never do it again," he said of his suicide attempt. What he learned at the New Vision Center for rehabilitation in St. Simon's Island, Georgia was that he'd been carrying around a "bucket" inside him which began to fill up with his troubles. Instead, while in rehabilitation, they made him carry around a teddy bear and the sight of this macho guy with a stuffed animal must have been a walking oxy-moron.

During all his troubled times, instead of pouring out the contents on occasion, Pell treated those woes like a trash compactor. Finally, the trash compactor blew up.

NCAA scandal aside, what a pity it would be for history revisionists to ignore Pell's contribution to Florida football.

"When you talk about the events that brought Florida to the fore as one of the most successful programs of the nineties," said Gene Peek, the Jacksonville attorney, former Gator Boosters president and president-elect of the Letterman's Club, "you have to include Charley Pell in there. Without him, there would have been no South end zone expansion and maybe no North end zone."

In addition to overhauling infrastructure, Pell probably did more to unite the various factions of fans around the state than any previous coach, bringing families and blue-collar types into the Gator inner circle.

As much as anyone, Pell was responsible for rebuilding the football facilities. Ben Hill Griffin Stadium ballooned up to 85,000, including posh luxury boxes, as a new era of Gator prosperity unfolded under Pell.

Having taken the job at Florida sight unseen when he arrived from Clemson, Pell was shocked to see the poor facilities at such a prestigious university.

And there was no money. Right off, he knew he had a big problem. There was going to be more to this than the job of coaching football. In fact, most of his energies in the first year would be devoted to the job of raising capital.

Small contributions weren't going to be enough. He needed a large cash infusion and had absolutely no idea where to get it.

Then along came his angel: Ben Hill Griffin Jr.

The grant of more than $25 million put Florida on the football map. You understand now why it's called Ben Hill Griffin Stadium.

"There was no way we could get it done unless we had a major benefactor," said Pell. "There are not very many people who could have done what he did."

How did it happen?

"We got introduced and--I'm going to take credit for this--I was smart enough not to push. I think he was figuring out how he felt about us. He invited us down to his Peace River Ranch. Let us go out and shoot turkeys. I just sat there on that back porch and rocked.

"He sat there and just figured. He asked questions that he wanted to ask. Damn, he was a tough guy to read. I could never tell what he was thinking.

"He'd ask a question and it might be three or four minutes before he'd ask another one. So having been around my grandpa, I learned to keep my mouth shut.

"Our relationship grew. And something encouraged him, made him want to do it. He was the benefactor that made it all happen."

Everything was in place for the explosion of Florida football on the national scene. Instead, it exploded in Charley Pell's face.

Pell also was the person who organized the first Gator Clubs around the state and preached pride to Gator fans, encouraging them to wear their colors proudly. "All you had to be," he said, "was a Gator. Period. Nothing else."

When you attend a Florida game today and see orange and blue shirts, hats, etc. on 90 per cent of the fans, it's because of Charley Pell. The idea first came when he took a trip to Tampa just after taking the job.

"I was walking along the route of the Gasparilla Parade--I guess it was about two miles--and I noticed that hardly anybody was wearing anything with 'Florida' on it," said Pell, who had just come to Gainesville.

"I'll bet you that I didn't see a dozen kids wearing the colors. And you can tell what the parents emphasize by what the kids are wearing. I knew right then we were in trouble."

He may have been obsessive/compulsive, but Charley Pell knew his color schemes: How to get people to wear orange and blue and how to get the supporters of he program to cough up the long green.

There were also a lot of bacon cheeseburgers and French fries that went into the early success of Florida's program. Because it was Dave Thomas, owner of Wendy's, who made the first big contribution to Florida under the Pell regime.

Dave's daughter, Wendy, after whom the chain is named, was a student at Florida.

"Mr. Thomas asked me how he could help," recalls Pell.

"I told him our weight room was about on par with most big high schools. He asked me how much it would take to fix it and I told him $50,000. He swallowed hard, and said, 'you got it.'"

There was a lot of sweat invested in that first year, most of it Pell's.

The first thing he had to do was ask a benefactor to help him build some new beds for the over-sized athletes in the athletic dorms. Cox furniture came to the rescue and customized them for the athletes. Peel feels that was a major accomplishment.

Then there had to be a new, modern, clean cafeteria.

"You have to start with where they live--where they eat and sleep--if you want to build pride in a team," said Pell.

It didn't always go so great, but Charley kept plugging away. "We could have done it a lot better. But I've never worked harder in my entire life. I can't remember ever stopping that first year."

Pell found out early that he could ask for something and quite often get it, including money from supporters to rebuild the sagging infrastructure. Part of the reason was that others saw how hard he was working.

"Charley Pell," says Florida athletic director Jeremy Foley, "taught me how to work. I thought I knew, but when Charley came along I found out how little I did know."

Years later, before the death of Ben Hill Griffin Jr., the billionaire from the tiny town of Frostproof, the University of Florida brass held a dinner in honor of the donor. Galen Hall was coach.

Griffin loved Florida football and was a courteous man. Yet when he was introduced and came to the podium, he started out his speech with: "I'm a Charley Pell man, myself."

Ben Hill Griffin never stopped being a Charley Pell man to the death. And Pell has never stopped being a Gator.

It grieves Pell to see Florida's lack of success against Florida State, which has taken advantage of the Gators' NCAA woes in the flesh market.

Only after five years of Spurrier did Florida begin to make up lost ground to FSU in the recruiting game.

"If that mess hadn't happened," Pell says of the probation, "Florida State would never have caught us."

Caught, as some would say, and passed the Gators.

It's true that FSU was a huge beneficiary of the cheating scandals at Florida, though certainly Florida's fault for breaking the rules in the first place.

What resulted after NCAA sanctions was a long drought for Florida football and it was then, along about the mid-eighties, that Bobby Bowden began to sign more blue chip players from the state than ever before.

It is also Pell's firm conviction that much of the information reported to the NCAA came out of the Seminoles' camp.

XIX. it's Free Shoes U. versus Probation U.

When the week finally rolled around for the 1994 meeting between the Florida Gators and Florida State University Seminoles, the anticipated combustion was rather slow in igniting.

Maybe because both teams had each lost one game and, with it, any reasonable chance for a national championship. Maybe because both coaches were trying to low-key the pre-game hype.

It certainly wasn't a harbinger of things to come.

Considering all that had transpired earlier that year between Spurrier and Florida State and his "Free Shoes University" comment about the shopping spree at Foot Locker by seven Seminole players, one would have expected some serious retaliation.

Where was all that "hate"? After all, it was "Hate Week." Good, clean hate. Not that destructive, kill-somebody-or-break-something kind of hate. But rather the competitive, I-wanna-kick-my-neighbor's-butt kind of hate. Hate the way Republicans hate Democrats and vice-versa. Florida-FSU Week.

'I wouldn't say this was hate. FSU-Florida is hate.'--Joe Gibbs

Somebody once asked former Washington Redskins coach Joe Gibbs the week of a big game with Dallas if the word "hate" accurately depicted the Redskins-Cowboys series. To which Gibbs, a former Seminole assistant coach, answered: "Hate? No, I wouldn't say that this is hate. FSU-Florida is 'hate.'"

Fifty weeks a year all residents take pride in the state of Florida boasting the best college football in the land with Florida, Florida State and Miami again ranking among the nation's elite.

Now it was time to choose sides again, just as it was Miami-FSU week when the Hurricanes knocked off the 'Noles.

As is usually the case, the three state schools were firmly entrenched in top 10 slots. The Associated Press ranked Florida No. 4, Miami No. 5 and FSU No. 7 (Colorado rated No. 6). The CNN-USA Today poll rated them the same, except FSU No. 6 ahead of Colorado.

The 1994 FSU-Florida game promised to be the closest game between the two state rivals played in at least four years and one of the most tightly contested of the past dozen. Although Florida held a huge 23-12-1 advantage in the series, FSU had dominated the past seven years, winning six times by a substantial average margin of more than 17 points.

As had been well-publicized in recent weeks following Florida's single loss to Auburn, Spurrier was 1-5 lifetime vs. the Bowdens, Bobby and Terry. Oddsmakers predicted it would be 1-6, since the Gators were an underdog for the first time this season. FSU was a three-point favorite despite the Gators' higher national ranking.

Spurrier, it seems, can never play against just one Bowden. He's got to play them both. You get Bobby, you get Terry.

ABC hooked up opposing FSU-Florida coaches for a live interview at halftime of the Nebraska-Oklahoma game on Friday after Thanksgiving.

There was Spurrier on the right side of the screen, and on the left were those Bowdens, Dad and Junior.

When Spurrier and his Gators arrived in Tallahassee for the game against FSU, there on one of the billboards advertising potato chips were those Bowden Boys again.

Isn't there a 15-yard penalty for too many head coaches from the same family on a billboard or the TV screen?

On one side it was "Free Shoes University," on the other "Probation U." The "Free Shoes" comment uttered by Spurrier at Gator Club meetings over the summer was just too delicious an opportunity for Spurrier to pass on.

After all, his alma mater had been bashed by FSU fans, as well as those of other rivals, for being placed on probation twice by the NCAA in the 1980s. Now it was going to be Florida State's turn in the barrel.

The eighties were tough times to be a Gator. Obviously tired of hearing about how he had been "out-recruited "by his state rival, Spurrier decided, as he often does, to take the offensive. That's when he endorsed the *Sports Illustrated* notion of possible wrong-doing by FSU and suggested the illegal inducements had influenced the decision of top recruits.

There were actually two parts to the story regarding Spurrier's quote. The "Free Shoes University" comment was jocular even to Bobby Bowden, who declined to get dragged into the dispute and, in fact, admitted that he makes "Gator jokes all the time" at Seminole Booster Club meetings.

"I'm a humorist," said Bowden, admitting that even he got a laugh out of it all.

Spurrier made the comment about "Free Shoes University" at several Gator Clubs.

But it was the two meetings in Lakeland and Orlando where the publicity caught up to him.

There wasn't much flap about his remark in Lakeland, although the quote was printed by the Lakeland Ledger. What did create a stir was what Spurrier told columnist Pete Kerasotis of *Florida Today* the next night.

Kerasotis had made the trip over from Melbourne to Orlando to interview Spurrier without even realizing what a bombshell he was about to explode.

That's when Spurrier said far more about the matter than he probably meant to, or that Kerasotis ever expected him to.

"It was clear to me that he wanted this out," said Kerasotis. "I gave him several chances to soften his position or maybe couch his words in a different manner, but he didn't want it. I think what happened is that he felt vindicated, because he'd been saying all along that it wasn't a level playing field when Florida recruited against Florida State."

In the Friday, June 10 edition of *Florida Today,* under the headline, *"But say I'm not surprised at what's happened. . .at FSU,"* Spurrier let loose on the Seminoles in an interview that was picked up by the national media.

"Maybe we're realizing why they've signed so many of those top players," Spurrier told the group in Orlando. And then he continued that theme in his interview with Kerasotis.

The *Sports Illustrated* story by Doug Looney, William F. Reed and Shelley Smith was just off the presses, charging that seven FSU players were implicated in the Foot Locker scandal as well as cash payments to six of the seven. Evidently it hit a familiar chord with Spurrier.

SI quoted defensive back Corey Sawyer, who had come out early in the NFL draft and signed with the Cincinnati Bengals in the fourth round, as saying of the shopping spree:

"We had about seven boxes of stuff. Big boxes. We were fitting about 12 winter coats in one box. We just bought out the Foot Locker, period."

Later, Sawyer would be indicted on perjury charges for lying under oath about his role in the shopping spree.

All that took place six days before the 1993 upset of Florida State by Notre Dame, according to *SI.* Spurrier wasted no time seconding the motion.

No, said Spurrier, he didn't believe that coach Bowden had known about the shopping spree, but that he was guilty of being "out of the loop."

"I believe some coaches try not to find out anything," he said. "I'm not mentioning any names, but some coaches deliberately stay out of the loop. This way, when something happens, they can say they've not done anything wrong."

All Spurrier asked, said Kerasotis, was that he not be portrayed as a whiner. "Don't make it sound like sour grapes or that I'm whining," he said to the writer. "because I'm not. But say that I'm not surprised as what happened up there at FSU."

More than any other point, he wanted Kerasotis to know that he'd suspected all along something was stunk in Tallahassee. "I've said these things before, so I don't know why people would be mad now. I guess it's just that before when I've said these things, nobody's paid attention. But now that Sports Illustrated has come out with these articles, people are paying attention.

"But, you know, this is not all new stuff. Go look at Sports Illustrated from last year when FSU played Notre Dame. It talks about how FSU players had better threads and wheels than Notre Dame players. Look it up."

There was a rumor circulating by mid-week that FSU fans planned to pelt the field at Doak Campbell Stadium with thousands of old sneakers, responding to Spurrier's "Free Shoes University" comment.

"I may have to wear a helmet or protection of some kind," Spurrier said after practice.

Neither stunt materialized. Maybe part of the reason was that Florida State fell behind so quickly and so badly that the Seminole fans were stunned into inaction.

FSU didn't score a touchdown until the fourth period and, by then, many disgruntled Seminole fans had left, missing what some would brand: "The Choke At Doak."

Regardless of the outcome of the 37th Florida-FSU game, the Seminoles would continue to suffer a bad image over the Foot Locker episode.

As Bowden had said: "The shoes were free, but we paid a heck of a price for it."

The 1994 Florida-FSU game was typically controversial, as has always been the case.

The two schools had feuded long before they played their first football game. If some members of the Florida Athletic Department would have had their way back in the fifties, the Gators would never have played the Seminoles in the first place.

It is not true that the Florida Legislature ordered the two schools to play each other, but it almost happened that way.

Florida had no intention of scheduling FSU, which had been known as Florida State College for Women until 1947. A bill in the state legislature that would have forced them to play failed on the Senate floor by a vote of 15-19 in April, 1955. Florida was forced to capitulate when Gov. LeRoy Collins gave the two schools' athletic directors 48 hours to work out the contract in 1957.

Ever since then, the air has fairly crackled with electricity in each of the 38 meetings between the Gators and Seminoles. Including that historic first game at Florida Field on Nov. 22, 1958.

The late Bobby Renn struck a huge blow for garnet and gold respect on the opening kickoff in the inaugural game. But for a brilliant defensive play by Florida's Jimmy Dunn, a fragile 145-pound quarterback/safety from Tampa, Renn would have returned it 92 yards for a touchdown.

I was sitting in the stands that day as a Florida student, one of 43,000 fans about to be startled by the opening play.

I marveled at both at the audacity of this renegade team from the panhandle as well as the nimble-footed Dunn. He back-pedaled half the field while fending off an FSU blocker to get a crack at Renn.

After the stunning reverse handoff from halfback Jack Espenship in a bit of Seminole trickery, FSU would go into score. You can imagine the shock waves at Florida Field after the very first series of plays!

"My job was to be the safety on the kickoff," Dunn recalled in the fall of '94 from the press box at Florida Field where he was scouting for the Tampa Bay Bucs, "and I did it extremely well, because I never would go down and mix it up on the kickoff. Just as the piles would go down, I was always standing next to them, but I was never in them."

The irony was that Dunn, an outstanding quarterback at Hillsborough High School in Tampa but not heavily recruited, had originally signed a one-year scholarship to play for Tom Nugent at FSU.

After running for two touchdowns and being named MVP in the 1955 Florida High School All-Star Game, Dunn signed a four-year grant with Florida, perturbing Nugent.

Though he would also run for two scores in Florida's 21-7 win over FSU that year, none of those TD would prove as impressive as Dunn's fighting off FSU blocker Bob Swoszowski and tackling Renn in the open field.

One could only speculate how it may have changed destiny had Renn not been stopped .

(Although the Seminoles would go on to score five plays later on Fred Pickard's' 1-yard run.)

"I think Bobby lost his patience," recalled Dunn, now a Tampa Realtor and coach of the Miami Hooters arena football team. "If he'd have just stayed behind his blockers, he would have backed me all the way out of the end zone."

Dunn would also eventually become a fellow assistant coach with Spurrier at Florida and later coach receivers for Spurrier's Tampa Bay Bandits.

Despite Florida's 21 unanswered points and the final 21-7 score in the inaugural game, I have often felt that Renn's runback made a statement on FSU's part that would never be repealed: Don't ever take us lightly again. And the Gators haven't.

Even after such a bombastic start, it would take FSU six more years to finally prevail in 1964.

The Seminoles did manage to nibble away at the Gators for the next few years, including a 3-3 tie in 1961 which brought down the goalposts at Florida Field.

It became painfully obvious to Florida faithful that under new head coach Bill Peterson that the gap was narrowing.

That's why in 1964 it was decided that the Gators should try a new psychological weapon: Jerseys bearing the inscription: "Go For Seven," the inference being that Florida State couldn't escape the Gators' mastery. If it was a mind game, then it failed.

One of the players on the first Florida team to be beaten by Florida State was sophomore quarterback Steve Spurrier.

"Coach (Gene) Ellenson had these jerseys made up that said 'Go For Seven,'" recalled Spurrier. "FSU people like to tell the story that it said, 'Never FSU, Never,' but it said 'Go For Seven.' Back in those days you could put whatever you wanted to on the jersey.

"So we all had those 'Go For Seven' shirts."

It was a game in which Steve Tensi hit Fred Biletnikoff over Allen Trammell on bomb and that play forevermore changed the conservative nature of this series.

"Tensi threw it 55-60 yards in the air. Trammel said he didn't think he could throw it that far. We fumbled down on their 1-yard line. Tommy Shannon started at quarterback and made a nice drive and just fumbled the snap at the one and they got it," said Spurrier.

Spurrier took over for Shannon in the second quarter, but it was 13-0 in the fourth period before he could get the Gators cranking. It would be the start of the Spurrier era at Florida, as a player.

The young sophomore quarterback made an impression that would lead to his role as a starter. He took them downfield on a long drive for a touchdown.

"(Jack) Harper scored on a little toss sweep from about eight yards out and now it's 13-7," said Spurrier. "Nine minutes left. And low and behold we tried an onside kick--one of the assistant coaches talked Coach (Ray) Graves into it."

FSU recovered, went on to add a Les Murdoch field goal and made history with its first victory over the Gators, 16-7.

Just as it was back in the days of Jimmy Dunn, Florida and FSU scrap hard over top high school recruits--but even moreso than ever. Time was 25 years ago when the Gators got their pick of blue-chippers in the state. Not anymore.

That intrastate recruiting war makes the Florida-FSU game even more competitive, because so many former high school teammates will be pitted against each other. Some even grow up wanting to attend one school or another and change their mind at the last second.

Such was the case with freshman running back sensation Elijah Williams of Milton, who never visualized himself in anything but garnet and gold.

And, according to FSU coach Bobby Bowden, it was also the case with Williams' freshman running back cohort, Fred Taylor of Belle Glade.

"I was always going to Florida State," said the red-shirt freshman Williams. "My mom was Florida State. My step-brother (running back Greg Allen) went to Florida State. I didn't even talk about Florida.

"'Until I had a Spanish teacher my senior year. She was a die-hard Gator fan. All she talked about was the Gators? Am I going to (play for) the Gators? 'Nah, I ain't goin' to the Gators.' Then I started thinking about schools and I took some visits and went to Florida.

"I didn't go to any parties or anything. It was just the atmosphere and the academics and stuff. And I knew I had an early chance to play. At Florida State I knew that they were looking at me as a defensive back, because I had played that my junior year and that's how they were recruiting me."

The Milton High Spanish teacher helped influence young Williams to visit Florida. She'd wear her Gator paraphernalia to school and address Elijah in his Spanish name, "Romeo."

"She'd said, 'what about those Gators, Romeo?'"

"And I'd say, 'I don't know.' She was always thinking about those Gators."

Williams' running mate, Taylor, did, in fact, commit to FSU, but later said he was pressured to do so and reneged to attend Florida. Taylor told Robbie Andreu of the *Gainesville Sun* that he was shocked by the angry response of Bobby Bowden when he informed the Seminoles coach that he had changed his mind. Bowden reportedly called the Belle Glade coach and expressed strong dissatisfaction.

"I guess you could say he (Bowden) questioned my manhood," said Taylor. "He said, 'You're going against your word.' I told him I had a right to change my mind. Then he said, 'you must be less of a man than I thought you were.'"

According to Taylor, he was informed on the Thursday before his visit to Florida that FSU only had "two or three scholarships left" and that he must give them an answer immediately. "I went ahead and told them I was going to give them a commitment," said Taylor.

Bowden claims, according to the *Sun*, that he had warned Taylor, "don't tell me unless you're coming." Bowden said he had planned to only sign one running back and that he was trying to tell Taylor he "had a responsibility and that he shouldn't go back on his word."

On the other side, FSU stars Derrick Alexander, Derrick Brooks and Devin Bush were on the bubble between the two schools and the Seminoles' 1990 victory over the Gators swung them over to the FSU side. Such are the recruiting wars in what is consider today the country's most talent-laden state.

FSU recruiting coordinator Ronnie Cottrell said that on virtually every player he recruits he is going up against Florida. He told Tom Spousta of the *Sarasota Herald-Tribune* that Spurrier was the biggest obstacle he had to overcome, especially with quarterbacks.

"Steve Spurrier has been a force in recruiting in Florida," said Cottrell. "He's the difference. He's the drawing card for their program. Every quarterback in the country I've talked to has some interest in him and his program."

Ironic that since Spurrier's reputation for coaching quarterbacks was so good, yet what he'd received the most criticism for at Florida was his coaching of Terry Dean, who was still buried in the never-never land of the Gator depth chart.

Spurrier felt the same way. He told *Sports Illustrated*: "It amazes me that I have to defend my track record. All these people are wondering if I still know how to coach quarterbacks."

Most people hoped that Terry Dean would surface one more time for Florida State. I did. So did some of the FSU players. Proving how little we know about the way Steve Spurrier was thinking.

XX. the FSU Lazaruses arise from the dead

On the eve of the 37th football game ever played between the Florida Gators and Florida State Seminoles, after a week of convincing myself FSU had a slight edge in Saturday's game, I woke up to a vision: "I think it's going to be a tie," I told my wife Joni as we stood on the porch of our Ocala home. "I just can't get a clear picture of either team winning."

Though not one to gamble on football, in retrospect I should have gotten on an airplane to Las Vegas right then and plunked down my inheritance on Florida as a 3-point underdog.

This only proves what I've always suspected: I am blessed with some sort of special psychic powers when it comes to college football.

TALLAHASSEE, FL, Nov. 26--Steve Spurrier doesn't beat a Bowden very often, but today he made up some lost ground.

--The Lead That Never Made
The New York Times

And especially when it comes to the Gators. Except whenever I brag about it, or if I were to bet on it. Or if I tell someone, fate reverses itself.

There are several exceptions about being clairvoyant. For one thing, your powers never work when used for the purpose of gambling.

Any public flaunting of these powers, such as making bold predictions on the radio or in the newspaper or telling too may people outside your immediate family circle, can be hazardous to your visionary status.

Most of all, never get out of the realm of your expertise. If you're an expert on colleges, *never* try picking the pros.

I once embarrassed myself on the NBC *Today Show*, telling Bryant Gumbel that the Denver Broncos would beat the Washington Redskins in the Super Bowl. In overtime.

Never mind how wrong that prediction was. You can look it up if you want to humiliate me.

Of course, by halftime of the Gator-Seminoles game I was beginning to feel a little insecure about my pick of a tie. And when the third quarter ended with Florida beating the bejabbers out of FSU, 31-3, I was hoping nobody would remember what I said.

There are comebacks and there are comebacks. This was The Ultimate Comeback.

Scoring a couple of touchdowns in the second half to win a game is really no mean feat. It's been done hundreds of times. I'd call that more of a rally.

You have to reach into biblical history to find some comparison and I guess Lazarus is as good as anybody, because he had been dead four days before Jesus brought him back to life. FSU was dead for three quarters.

Florida State's 1994 Seminoles pretty much played like Lazarus. This was a monster rally, one that Seminole fans would ever forget. Neither would Gator fans.

If the Gator faithful ever had a tendency to be schizophrenic, then this game would put them into deep shock therapy, because it definitely had two different personalities.

For three quarters, Steve Spurrier's team looked invincible. It was remarkable how "vincible" they became in the final period.

This would go down as the Gators' biggest fourth-quarter collapse of all time and one of the biggest in college football history, which is why Seminole fans have since named it "The Choke At Doak."

It was definitely not a day for the media to be drawing any early conclusions. Brent Musburger and Dick Vermeil of ABC had already ordained the Gators as national championship contenders and "maybe the best team we've seen all year."

They weren't alone, however, because you could almost feel the pending doom hanging over the collective heads of Seminole fans in Doak Campbell Stadium. At least what was left of them. Some had already departed their seats, having accepted their bitter pill. They never read about Lazarus.

I happened to be covering the game for the *New York Times*, that day, writing a "running" account for the early edition.

A "running" is built paragraph-by-paragraph as the game unfolds. As soon as you have reached some logical point in the second half where you can see a distinct trend developing, you begin scratching out your lead paragraphs, leaving the score blank until the game ends.

With Florida trouncing FSU, 31-3, as the fourth quarter began, there was a fairly strong trend, wouldn't you say?

So this is the lead graf I wrote which had to be scrubbed and never made it into the New York Times:

"TALLAHASSEE, FL, Nov. 26--Steve Spurrier doesn't beat a Bowden very often, but today he made up some lost ground."

That one wound up in the scrap heap.

Not only would this angle fail to hold up, but what unfolded in the next few minutes was perhaps the most classical reversal of momentum I had ever witnessed in my 35 years of covering sporting events for newspapers and TV.

And, for a print reporter with a deadline, it would prove to be a frantic post-game journalistic exercise of Clark Kent parameters.

For this game to ultimately wind up tied 31-31 is like waking up in Florida on a July morning to discover a foot of snow on the ground. Another deal like the Dewey-Truman headline in the Chicago Tribune. This kind of stuff just doesn't happen.

The assault began with what seemed to be a harmless touchdown with just under 13 minutes left to play and Florida head 31-10.

If anybody besides Seminole quarterback Danny Kanell thought it possible for FSU to score three more touchdowns and nearly get into position for a winning field goal, then they ought to be required to take a lie detector test.

At one point in the second half, Bowden had even suggested to quarterback coach Mark Richt that Kanell ought to be benched. To his credit, Richt didn't concur.

For sure Bobby Bowden didn't believe there was enough time for his team to make it all the way back, because he admitted it.

For sure Spurrier and defensive coordinator Bob Pruett didn't, either.

For sure I didn't, because until the fourth Seminole TD, I hadn't even remotely considered that I would have to start re-writing my lead.

My plan was simple: Finish the story before the game was over, grab the elevator down to the locker rooms, select a few choice quotes, zip back up to the press box and insert them in my story and file the first of two stories to the New York Times before 4 p.m. EDT.

So much for hindsight about foresight.

Nothing seemed to work well that day, including Florida's fourth-quarter defense. . .as well as the elevator from high atop Doak Campbell to the ground floor. When the game ended, writers were scrambling out of every exit, trying to find some method of descending to the locker room.

It was 3:30 p.m. By now it was fairly obvious I wasn't going to make my *Times* deadline. Just then, the elevator light came on and I could see it was working again as it headed back up to the press box. The sports department clerk in New York picked up the phone at precisely the same time.

"Please tell Jay Schreiber I can't make this first deadline," I said frantically. "I'm on my way to the locker room."

Before I could say anything else, he had switched me over to the copy desk and a woman named Kathleen.

"We've got to have a story," she said.

"I can't do it Kathleen, or I'll miss the press conferences in the locker room."

"You've got until 4:40. We've *got* to have it by then."

"OK," I said, somewhat relieved that I'd been granted an extra 40 minutes. "I'll have it there."

By now the elevator had gone. I sprinted out the side door and began to work my way down through the stadium seats, through the crowd, which had thinned out. I finally got there and back. And my second-edition story made it to New York. It read like this:

FROM: BUDDY MARTIN, DOAK CAMPBELL
FLORIDA-FSU WRITETHRU

By BUDDY MARTIN

Special To The New York Times

TALLAHASSEE, FL, Nov. 26--They don't play overtime in Division 1A college football. And for that, Steve Spurrier and the Florida Gators can be thankful.

Had there been any more ticks left on the Doak Campbell Stadium clock, smart money says the Florida State Seminoles would have probably beaten the Gators instead of winding up in a 31-31 tie.

As it was, FSU rode the arm of quarterback Danny Kanell to a 28-point rally that rivaled the greatest fourth-quarter comeback in major college history, Washington State's 28-point rally against Stanford in 1984.

Kanell got the ball back with 22 seconds left and, after two completions, was scrambling frantically for a clock-stopping first down when he was tackled a yard short by Gator safety Michael Harris. The game ended at the Gator 43. It was only the second tie in 37 football games between these two cross-state rivals.

The largest crowd ever to see a game here, 80,210, watched the most dramatic finish in series history as both teams completed the regular season 9-1-1.

The Seminoles' Bobby Bowden considered the tie a moral victory. And Spurrier felt like he had salvaged just enough dignity to keep his team afloat for next week's Southeastern Conference title game.

Florida goes against unbeaten, No. 3 ranked Alabama, with the winner going to the Sugar Bowl.

"We've been talking about that game since the beginning of spring practice, trying to get to Atlanta and play for the championship," said Spurrier. "This is not an end-of-the-season game for us."

Atlantic Coast Conference champion FSU's post-season fate is yet to be determined.

Bowden felt he'd gotten a reprieve.

"I've never had a tie feel as much like a win," Bowden said. "As we were moving down the field, I kept thinking, 'there's not enough time.' I couldn't believe it could happen."

Neither could Spurrier. He was just grateful that Bowden didn't go for the two-point conversion after the Seminoles' fourth touchdown and said he "probably would have" had he been in that situation.

"I guess I ought to feel fortunate they didn't go for two," said Spurrier. "A tie is a tie. It's better than a loss."

Bowden said he opted for the Dan Mowrey PAT kick because he wanted to put the pressure back on Florida.

"I went for one because I didn't want to lose after coming back the way we did," said Bowden.

"I thought I would put the pressure back on them (Florida) and let them gamble with the football.

"And it almost worked."

Indeed, FSU had come from afar.

Florida was brilliant early, with sophomore quarterback Danny Wuerffel throwing three first-half touchdowns--two of them to junior All-American wide receiver Jack Jackson-- as the Gators went up 24-3 at the half.

Wuerffel, on his way to perhaps a career day, scored Florida's fourth touchdown afoot in the third period to put his team up 31-3.

Wuerffel also posted impressive numbers with 304 yards passing.

But in the clutch, with Jackson on the sideline in the second half with a pulled hamstring, the Gators appeared to pull in the reins in favor of the running game.

Kanell, on the other hand, played bombs away, passing for 421 yards, engineering four last-period TD drives, on his way to a possible winning field goal drive when he ran out of time.

In the final 13 minutes, Kanell masterfully quarterbacked drives of 84, 60, 73 and 60 yards.

Only one of the four scores came on a Kanell pass, a 6-yarder to wide receiver Adrian Cooper. Clearly, however, Kanell's passing fueled them all.

The other FSU scores were on short runs by fullback Zack Crockett, Kanell and Rock Preston.

Kanell, booed at home sometimes this season after inheriting the job from departed Heisman Trophy winner Charlie Ward, almost didn't survive the second half to make history.

Bowden said he and his assistant coaches discussed benching the 6-4, 215-pound junior quarterback from Fort Lauderdale but decided against it.

Kanell also suffered a slight concussion with just over seven minutes to play in the third quarter.

"I guess," Kanell said, making a play on words, "you could say I played 'unconscious' in the second half."

Unconscious, indeed. Of his 421 yards passing, Kanell rolled up 349 of them in the second half during which he completed 34 of 40 passes.

The play of the game for FSU came on a run by Warwick Dunn after catching a short Kanell pass with about three minutes left.

Looking as though he would step out of bounds, Dunn tight-roped the sideline past two Gator defenders and turned what appeared to be a short gain into a brilliant piece of running for 37 yards to the Florida 23. From there, FSU scored in five plays on Crockett's run.

"Warwick Dunn may be the best scatback in the country," said Spurrier. "We had two guys with an angle, he gave them both a limp shoulder and he was off."

Neither team had much hopes for a national championship without a loss by No. 1 ranked Nebraska or No. 2 Penn State.

Florida had entered the game ranked No. 4 in both polls. FSU was No. 6 in the Associated Press poll, No. 7 in the Coaches' Poll.

"Our hopes for a national championship were pretty slim anyway," said Spurrier.

Florida's lone defeat was against another Bowden-coached team, Auburn, 36-33. With the loss to Bobby's son, Terry, and the tie against FSU, Spurrier is now 1-5-1 lifetime against the Bowdens.

Florida State's lone defeat was 34-20 by Miami.

On what turned out to be one of the most devastating days of his coaching career, Steve Spurrier stood tall in the wake of virtual disgrace. There are those who are want to criticize him for being overly sensitive and thin-skinned, but Spurrier withstood this heat with asbestos-like skin.

The smaller things that might cause team dissension drive him nuts, but he is usually equal to the task in a crisis.

Nothing like this had ever happened in Florida football, and especially under Steve Spurrier's watch.

There was a time in 1962 that Ray Graves' team hammered Duke for a 21-0 halftime lead and then watched Coach Bill Murray bring his Blue Devils back for four second-half touchdowns in a 28-21 victory.

Murray's son-in-law, Bill Donigan of Gainesville, tells the story that the Duke coach simply stood at the door of the locker room and asked "everybody who thinks we can come back and win shake my hand." Every Duke player complied. The Blue Devils came roaring back.

Then there was the infamous 1965 Sugar Bowl game against Missouri in which Florida was on the short end of a comeback led by a junior quarterback named Steve Spurrier.

Badly manhandled by the Tigers for three quarters and trailing 20-0 in what seemed more like 56-0, the Gators had been virtually unable to move the ball for three quarters.

Using his own ingenuity and making up some plays, Spurrier took Florida in for a score. Gator coaches, fearing that they were under fire for the Gators' lack of offense, decided they would go for two points. Offensive Coordinator Ed Kensler would say: "20 to 8 looks better than 20 to 6."

The try for two failed. Moments later, Spurrier had his team in the end zone again. This time it was obvious Florida needed to try for two points. Failed again. Now it was 20-12. And yes, when the Gators scored a third touchdown in the final period, it was obvious what had to be done.

And it's obvious what happened, with the final score Missouri 20, Florida 18. It doesn't take a math genius to tell us that three kicks would have won the Sugar Bowl for Florida.

There were so many crucial plays in that fourth period of the '94 Florida-FSU game that it's difficult to separate them.

None will be more scrutinized that Danny Wuerffel's interception with just four minutes to play, which produced flashbacks from the Auburn game six weeks earlier.

Wuerffel and freshman receiver Reidel Anthony are supposed to make reads together as the play unfolds, but the quarterback anticipated an outside move and the freshman went inside. Result: Seminole corner back James Colzie made a spectacular diving interception that would lead to FSU's tying touchdown, the four-yard plunge by running back Rock Preston.

It was a play that will haunt Gator fans forever. And another one of those cursed interceptions that drives Spurrier into fits of insomnia.

After FSU, there was also great potential for Florida's season to go South, right down the drain.

Spurrier had to put on a good face on the outcome, turning his attention to next week's SEC title game against Alabama in Atlanta. It would take all of his coaching acumen.

This game was virtually locked away in the Gators' vault and the safecrackers from Florida State stole. Anytime anybody in the future ever criticizes Spurrier for running up the score, all he need say is: "Remember FSU."

With your team ahead 31-3 and 13 minutes left to play in the game, if you can't consider that a safe lead, then nothing will ever be safe again. "It just goes to show you," Spurrier said after the game, "you can never have too many points."

Later, Spurrier would look back at the first FSU game and say: "Obviously, we'd do something different if played that game over (with a 31-3 lead). They just got in the shotgun and threw the ball. We couldn't stop them and we couldn't make first downs. We couldn't even make them go the 'slow route.'"

Spurrier had to address post-game comments by Gator players directed at defensive coordinator Bob Pruett's scheme. Those remarks by such leaders as defensive lineman Ellis Johnson and defensive back Larry Kennedy were not smiled upon kindly.

In the end, the Gators had a "prayer meeting" among themselves and out of it came an even greater sense of resolve.

Alas, though, a minor miracle happened. Because there wasn't another opponent as worthy as FSU, the Seminoles accepted a bid to play the Gators in the USF&G Sugar Bowl. They called it "The Fifth Quarter" and "The Overtime Bowl."

Although Spurrier says he did not dangle the "Florida State carrot" out to his players for incentive to beat Alabama, he didn't have to, because he knew how badly they wanted to win an SEC title, as well as another crack at the Seminoles.

XXI. the way Spurrier counts it's *FOUR*

Steve Spurrier was holding up four fingers as the publicist from the Southeastern Conference was introducing the Florida coach for his post-game press conference down in the innards of the Georgia Dome in Atlanta.

"Steve Spurrier has become the first SEC coach to win three conference titles outright in his first five years," he said.

That's when Spurrier flashed the four fingers, like a kid making a signal behind the back of the teacher, to nobody in particular among the media folk.

To his critics, such a gesture by Spurrier would have appeared arrogant, but those who took the time to listen and understand would have realized that was not the case at all.

In fact, the four fingers were symbolic of the loyalty Spurrier feels for his very first Gator squad which blazed the way in 1990 for the future success of his teams.

He was counting the one they took away not for his own personal pride, but for his players. Because of infractions under Galen Hall's regime, his '90 squad wasn't eligible for an SEC title or a bowl game.

Having only won the championship once, under Charley Pell in 1984, and then having it stripped because of NCAA sanctions, Florida was therefore still without an SEC trophy on its mantle back then.

'It's just a shame the 1990 team was ineligible.'--Steve Spurrier

Though Spurrier's '90 team couldn't technically claim the title, he wanted it known that they were a part of this championship.

"It's just a shame that the 1990 team was ineligible to be called champions because of an alleged violated that happened in 1986. None of those players or coaches were involved in any wrong-doing," said Spurrier.

"And for those guys to be denied the championship when they really won it is an injustice."

Spurrier made a vow that if his '90 team did have the best record, "we'd recognize them along with our other SEC champions." And he kept that promise.

That, I felt, was a generous act by Spurrier. And so when I did an interview the next day on *Dave Kirvin's Sunday Sports Desk* on *Sports Radio Network*, I felt the need to come to Spurrier's defense somewhat.

It was worthy of mentioning that Spurrier and losing coach Gene Stallings sort of reversed roles. Spurrier, the so-called arrogant one, had been a gracious winner. Stallings, the Southern gentleman, had acted like a jerk.

History shows us now that Spurrier out-coached his Alabama counterpart badly in the final period. That's not a popular theme in the state of Alabama, as I found out from the irate callers to *American Sports Radio* following my critical comments of Stallings. But it was a true statement.

Here is an edited and updated version of the story I wrote the next day from Atlanta for the *Ocala Star-Banner*:

ATLANTA--On the first December Sunday morning in Georgia, less than a dozen hours after one of the truly remarkable football games in Gator football history, middle-aged Florida fans awakened to a day they never thought they'd see in their lifetimes:

A football dynasty proclaiming their team's dominance over the Southeastern Conference.

Such a radical notion as this about a decade ago would have been considered as preposterous as thinking the Republicans would own a majority in Congress in 1995.

Welcome to the world of the impossible.

With apologies to my sports writing brethren, who have no doubt used these parodies on clichés in many stories before me:

Hell has frozen over, the cows have come home and the fat lady's voice is beginning to sound sweeter to Florida football fans than Barbra Streisand, Reba McIntyre and Whitney Houston all put together.

Florida has won the SEC football championship. Again. The only teams for the first 50 years of the conference never to own a league title were Florida and Vanderbilt. The Gators have now claimed two straight and three in four years.

Hold it! Make that four, says Spurrier, holding up four fingers at his post-game press conference after the Gators' 24-23 victory in the SEC championship game Saturday.

What's this? Can't he count? Is the guy THAT greedy?

The much-maligned, often-unappreciated and inappropriately nicknamed "Evil Genius" Steve Spurrier is pleading with the media:

Don't forget my 1990 team that went 6-1 to post the best SEC record, but wasn't eligible due to NCAA probation.

The five-year transformation which lead to the resurrection of Gator football from the ashes can be directly laid at the feet of Stephen Orr Spurrier. The Prodigal not only brought home championship rings, but restored dignity to his alma mater.

Today I think of all those long-suffering Gator fans who pledged allegiance to their team through rain and sleet and snow and drought, some of whom never lived to see the sunshine.

I think especially of my late brother-in-law, Armand Lovell of Ocala, a Florida graduate and avowed Gator fan who was alive to see the 1984 team win it and lose it. And he was around for the 1990 mythical SEC title, but not the others.

I think of Gary Peacock, a Tampa attorney friend and Florida journalism classmate who dropped dead this year in a charity walk-a-thon and always kept me abreast of Gator happenings by sending newspaper clippings.

And of so many others, still alive, like Whit Palmer Jr., Red Mitchum, Fred Montsdeoca, Gene Peek III, Wayne McCall, Dutton Long, Augie Greiner, Bart Kimball, Jimmy Stellogeannis, Vic and Gus Musleh, Tommy Herren, etc. for whom Sunday was one of those Great Gettin'-Up Gator Mornings.

For those, and all other long-suffering Gator fans, I chose these freeze frames to live for an eternity in my own personal time capsule:

■Danny Wuerffel, coming off the field after having thrown his third interception this year in the fourth quarter of a big game, allowing Alabama to take a 23-16 lead with just under nine minutes to play. Florida's best offensive player, wide receiver Jack Jackson, is gone with a shoulder injury and its second half offense is lost in space.

Here, in the devastation of the moment which certainly qualified as the season's low point, Wuerffel finds the courage to clap his hands and tell his down-trodden, dispirited coach: "Don't worry, we'll get it back." And then he goes out and does it.

■The sheer genius--not the "evil genius" tag one Atlanta sports writer hangs on him--of Spurrier that unfolds over the next 10 plays, including the delicious fake injury by Wuerffel, the "Double Pass" and the Emory & Henry formation. Gene Stallings' defense was snookered when Wuerffel limped off the field, Eric Kresser rushed out to take the snap. Before anybody could ever detect the change, Kresser had completed a 25-yarder to freshman Ike Hilliard. Then comes the "Double Pass" of Wuerffel to Chris Doering to Aubrey Hill that carried to Alabama's two, whereupon Wuerffel so skillfully checks off from a quarterback sneak and hits Doering on a slant for the TD. A classic drive to be savored, but one that Spurrier says was born out of desperation.

"Nothing else was working and we had to try something different," he said.

Different, indeed. But it may have been Spurrier's finest offensive series at Florida.

■The arrogance of losing coach Gene Stallings, offended that writers would have the audacity to ask why he didn't go for the two-point conversion when he led by five points. High school coaches know that the rule in that situation is you must go for two.

Stallings apparently thinks he plays by a different set of rules. Spurrier, the beneficiary of decisions by coaches eschewing the two-pointer two straight weeks, says he would have gone for the deuce, because "that's what the chart says."

Ironically, in somewhat of a role reversal, it was Spurrier, accused of being an ego-driven hothead, as the gracious winner. And Stallings, with his alleged Southern gentleman's grace, as the sore loser. Gene Stallings is a terrific football coach, but he is not above criticism and he is not Bear Bryant re-incarnated. Bear Bryant wouldn't have kicked.

Spurrier outcoached his Alabama counterpart. But he also knows a blessing when he sees one. "God certainly smiled on the Gators today," Spurrier had said in the opening comment of his press conference.

Actually, Spurrier could have stopped right there. Everything else was superfluous.

Except, perhaps, for holding up those four fingers in a proper and gracious tribute to those pioneers who trail-blazed the path to SEC supremacy.

What the story did not say was that in addition to leaving the room in a huff with writers, Stallings had also encountered SEC Commissioner Roy Kramer as he walked off stage and yelled at the Commissioner's for his choice of officials to work that game.

Obviously, Stallings felt his Alabama team had gotten the worst end of the calls. In the NFL, he would have been hit with a big fine.

Understandably, Alabamans are getting tired of losing title games to Florida. The callers from that state to Dave Kirvin's show, responding to my remarks about Stallings' sour grapes, didn't take kindly to my theme.

One kid wanted to know how Spurrier could claim the 1990 title and, if he was going to, why couldn't Terry Bowden claim the 1993 title, since Auburn was on probation? It was a slightly different situation, of course, because back in 1990 when Spurrier's team finished 6-1 with the best record in the conference, there *was* no SEC title game.

And in order to have claimed the 1993 title, Auburn needed to win that post-season game which it wasn't eligible for, even though Auburn had beaten both of its participants, Auburn and Florida.

Another Alabaman--"Hal from Florence" I believe it was--called the show to ask how a guy writing a book about Florida had the right to comment about Gene Stallings' post-game demeanor. The guy writing the book wanted to know how Hal from Florence could explain Stallings' behavior when he wasn't even in attendance at the post-game press conference.

People, I guess, see things as they want to see them.

In retrospect, with a few weeks to look back on the SEC title game, the defining moment of the season and maybe one of the pivotal points of several years to come happened right there on the sideline after the Wuerffel interception.

Florida had been developing a reputation for losing close games and, in fact, dissension was mounting on the team between the offense and defense. That interception was the catalyst.

Just how Wuerffel was able to extrapolate himself from the jaws of failure at that moment remains one of the true folk tales of Spurrier's regime at Florida.

Remember, now, that Spurrier had benched a leading Heisman Trophy candidate just six weeks prior in favor of Wuerffel.

And it was Wuerffel--not Terry Dean--who had thrown killer interceptions in the loss to Auburn and the tie with Florida State.

Now Wuerffel would throw another costly interception, this one against Alabama with 8:56 to play (although it was a tipped pass).

As Wuerffel broke the huddle on second and 10 dropped back to pass, the ensuing few seconds were about the break the collective hearts of Gator fans once again. His pass to Aubrey Hill was bobbled, bounced off the helmet of Cedric Samuel and right into the hands of freshman linebacker Dwayne Rudd of Batesville, Mississippi.

In a flash Rudd was in the end zone, Alabama had a 22-17 lead and it was time for the Tide to launch the extra point.

Truth be known, these events may have stunned even Stallings, for the decision he was about to make would eliminate any real chance he was going to have of winning the game or the SEC.

Such an unfortunate fate fit the pattern of a season when Florida had frittered away its first real chance for a national championship because of the inability to take care of business in the closing minutes of key games. There was the last three minutes of infamy against Auburn, the 12:59 of hell against Florida State and now the 8:56 in Atlanta that could have changed the entire complexion of the season.

"How about it," Malcom Moran of the New York Times had asked me at that point. "Can Florida come back?"

I had to reflect for a moment before I answered Moran. "Yes," I said, "I think they can."

The real character of 1994 Gator team and its coaching staff was about to unfold in the next few minutes down there on the floor of the Georgia Dome. Nursing a 17-16 lead over Alabama with 9:07 to play when they got the ball back at their own 17, it was up to Wuerffel and coach.

I scribbled in my notebook: "It's up to Spurrier and the offense here to win it." That was half right.

On one hand the Gators couldn't be foolish--as they were in the final moments against Auburn--and on the other they couldn't get too conservative with so much time left.

Meanwhile, instead of going for the two-point play with his team up by five points, Stallings would elect to kick. It seemed to me that Stallings was caught off-guard and instinctively went for the PAT.

"A lot of times it's just sort of automatic that the kicking team runs on the field and you really don't think that much about it," said Spurrier. "I think that's probably what happened. I really wasn't thinking about it at the time either. I didn't even watch because I was over there trying to get some ball plays ready, talking to Danny and the offensive guys.

"Obviously I don't think they stopped and thought about it deeply, or they would have gone for two in that situation."

Later, Stallings would try to explain it away by saying he didn't want to get beat by two field goals, which really didn't make a lot of sense if you know Spurrier's attacking style on offense.

If Stallings didn't know, he was about to find out in the next three minutes, 17 seconds of playing time with Florida down 23-17.

Of such stuff heroes are made. Two of them were about to emerge, three if you count Spurrier. One of them the unlikeliest of heroes.

One, Wuerrfel trotted off the field clapping his hands and as he passed Spurrier, remarked: "Don't worry about it coach, we'll get it back!"

In the deepest, darkest corner of his career, this young man had found some kind of light which was calling him through to the other side of the tunnel.

About the same time, all hell was breaking loose among the Florida defense on the sideline. Blows were about to be exchanged between safety Lawrence Wright and tackle Henry McMillian, who had lashed out at the offense for turning the ball over in a crucial situation.

First, defensive lineman Kevin Carter got in between them and he nearly duked it out with McMillian, his good friend.

That's when Ron Zook stepped up. Zook, the forgotten man, who was unceremoniously demoted as Florida's defensive coordinator after the 1993 season, whose job was taken by Bob Pruett. Ron Zook, now merely the special teams and nickel backer coach. He called the defense together and told the players they had a lot of nerve blaming the offense and demanded they get focused on the task at hand.

Zook told the defense the game was not over yet, that the offense was going to score and that the game could be won by stopping Alabama on the last drive.

Coincidence or not, the Florida Gators would proceed to go out and play maybe their best defensive series of the year.

Imagine, however, the sheer dejection of the moment for Spurrier.

The Gator coach looked like he wanted to barf up his lunch on the sideline.

And what of Wuerffel, who was now about to have the goat horns pinned on him for the third time in three games which Florida failed to win?

Their backs to the wall, Spurrier told his quarterback: "We're going to spread and try something different."

That's when Spurrier threw the trick-bag at Alabama.

What transpired was one of the finest drives of the Spurrier era at Florida--one that advocates of illusion will long remember: 80 yards and a millennium of sorcery.

On the second play, Spurrier pulled off a shocker from which Alabama was never able to recover: The Fake Gimp Quarterback Play.

Having been tackled on a pass attempt, Wuerffel limped off the field, faking a leg injury, and sophomore Eric Kresser--he of the big-time arm--rushed on. Wuerffel appeared injured to even the biggest of cynics.

Everybody knows the coach's manual says that when a new quarterback comes in the game after an injury, common sense dictates that he'll just hand the ball off.

Instead, Kresser dropped to pass--a deep route--and got almost no rush from the Tide defenders. So wide open was Ike Hilliard that even though the ball was underthrown, nobody was near the Gator receiver. It was a 25-yard gain.

Sparse though the running yards might have been for Florida, freshman Taylor earned his scholarship with a carry for the most critical yard of his life on fourth and one.

He was stopped, but Taylor kept bucking until he penetrated the plane for the first down.

Now came the cock-eyed formation Spurrier nicknamed the "Emory & Henry" after the tiny Virginia school where it allegedly originated: A triangle or "trips" to one side and twins to the other side with no running back and the quarterback under center.

Ironically, when Florida tried this the first time, defensive coordinator Bill Oliver of Alabama quickly called time out.

Actually, the 'Bama coach had seen this formation when he was coaching for Pepper Rodgers and the Memphis Showboats in the USFL days. Spurrier ran it against him as head coach of Tampa Bay.

This time, it was more the beauty of play sequence than one play itself, which is the true genius of Spurrier anyway. He sets you up for a left hook and then hits you with a right cross, then hits you with a left hook. So when Wuerffel threw a sideways lateral/pass to Reidel Anthony for a 9-yard gain, Alabama seemed to be relieved that it hadn't gone for more. Let's hear it for damage control!

Who would have thought Spurrier would have come back on the very next play with another Emory & Henry variation? So we'll call this one The Emory & Henry Deja Vu:

Chris Doering was the target of the lateral, but instead of running as had Anthony, Doering faked the run and then heaved it down field to Aubrey Hill at the Crimson Tide 2. That double-pass was Spurrier's favorite call of the year and maybe his best, too.

As long as Wuerffel had them on the ropes, he lined up for Spurrier's call of a quarterback sneak, audibled and used Doering as a receiver for the winning touchdown.

"And then Alabama 'consumed the clock' for us," Spurrier said, chuckling in wonderment to himself at the notion that the Tide would come out so conservatively when it needed to score and play into the hands of the Gator defense, which was about to stage one of its best stands of the year.

This was perhaps the finest back-to-back, one-two punch by the offense and defense of Spurrier's first five years at Florida.

The front four, especially Kevin Carter and Ellis Johnson, were dominant.

So dominant that Johnson was named the game's Most Valuable Player, even though a defensive player. How often does that happen to a Steve Spurrier team?

Johnson said later that he and his unit just "willed" the defensive stand which was highlighted by the spectacular tip of a Jay Barker pass by defensive back Fred Weary to kill off 'Bama's hopes.

All things considered, this proved to be one of Florida's greatest football victories in school history, especially considering the conference championship was at stake.

And after the FSU fiasco, this game could have been full of land mines for Spurrier. So his brilliant offensive strategy and the defensive spurt in the final minutes proved an unbeatable combination.

Remember, too, the division between the coaching staff and players, as well as the offense and defense, which had reared its ugly head the week before in the 31-31 tie with Florida State. That's why Zook's sideline intervention was key, although Spurrier downplayed the sideline problem.

It says something, too, that Ellis Johnson, who had been chewed out for complaining about the defensive scheme in the FSU comeback, stepped up big-time as MVP.

The following week Zook received an offer to become the defensive coordinator for new Michigan State coach Nick Saban. He went in Spurrier's office to tell him he was leaving.

Spurrier asked Zook to change his mind and offered him the position of "assistant head coach."

Receivers coach Dwayne Dixon was also named "assistant head coach," taking the spot of Charlie Strong, who joined Lou Holtz's staff at Notre Dame. Quarterbacks coach John Reaves had gone to South Carolina as offensive coordinator.

In few days, Zook accepted the new title. He didn't really get his old job back of defensive coordinator, because Bob Pruett still occupies that, but he moved up one notch in the pecking order.

Whether or not Zook's was a battlefield promotion was difficult to confirm one way or another.

However, Zook's decision to stay would prove popular with those who knew him as an enthusiastic, dedicated aide. And Spurrier, who had demoted Zook a year prior, perhaps had righted his wrong.

I wondered if somehow that meant he would also patch up things with Terry Dean before it was over. After all, there was still the Sugar Bowl to go, Dean's last game as a Gator.

Looking back, said Spurrier he made the correct choice in starting Danny Wuerffel after the loss to Auburn.

"We did the right thing, what was best for the team, changing quarterbacks," he said. "No question."

Though Dean said in early spring of 1995 that he has no hard feelings for Spurrier, there is clearly a psychological residue and it has left marks on the both of them. In addition, the rift has caused hard feelings between Spurrier and Dean's father, Frank, who reportedly blames Spurrier for his son not getting drafted.

"Shane Matthews (Bears) didn't get drafted, either," said Spurrier.

Over the years I have witnessed many confrontations between quarterback and coach--especially in the pros.

John Elway had a role in the dismissal of Denver Broncos head coach Dan Reeves.

Terry Bradshaw, late in his career, fought openly with the coach for whom he won four Super Bowls, Chuck Noll. The two of them still don't speak.

Spurrier, himself, wasn't all that fond of Tampa Bay Bucs head coach John McKay, who ultimately cut him. McKay didn't think Spurrier threw enough passes to his son, Jon, a wide receiver.

I offered the traditional coach/quarterback dispute up as a possible correlation between Spurrier and Dean. The Gator coach didn't buy into that scenario. He kept playing that old tape.

"One individual. . .I don't think you can say that happens a lot," said Spurrier. "Terry is the one quarterback that I admit, I've done a poor job of coaching. I said, 'I can't get him to play the way we'd like for him to.' When I couldn't get him playing the way I wanted to, then you play the other player."

Then he reverted back to his standard remarks about Dean, trying to be a diplomat: "I don't want to say anything about Terry Dean. I've had good relationships with all my quarterbacks, but for some reason Terry was difficult for me to coach.

"If he goes on to the NFL and has a great career, then he can blast me and say I handled him very poorly. If he doesn't do all that, then maybe he should say, 'I was fortunate to do all that I did here at Florida.' And he had a wonderful career.

"But unfortunately, I guess he thought we were supposed to win the national championship and he was supposed to win the Heisman and it didn't work out. His expectations may have been to high.

"I tried to coach him the best I could. But obviously I can coach those other guys a little bit better. Seems like they play within our system a little bit better than Terry."

Clearly, Spurrier felt like there had been a breach between him and Dean after the Auburn game, when Dean revealed he had been "on probation," so to speak.

"After the Auburn game I took up for him," said Spurrier. "I said, 'I had a lot of bad plays called. I didn't have as good a plays for him as maybe Danny had.' So I gave him a little bit of an out there, as I try to do with all our guys when they have a rough game.

"When he got on the band wagon to say I put too much pressure on him, then that's not what I want to ever do to any player--even if it's the left guard or a receiver. If they sense there's too much pressure on them then, again, I've done a lousy job of coaching them."

In retrospect, maybe Dean was a product of a system which prematurely vaulted him into the national limelight and, in the end, Dean could no longer sustain. The fast start against New Mexico State--seven touchdowns in the first half--might have given Dean a reputation that he couldn't live up to.

"Who's to say," said Spurrier, "that some of those other quarterbacks couldn't have thrown seven? But nobody knows that."

But because he elected to make the change, Spurrier was accused by some of holding a personal grudge. As so often is the case in these kinds of disputes, nobody really wins. And, worst yet, all that you have accomplished together as player and coach over five years is soon forgotten, obliterated by bitterness and resentment.

XXII. sly old fox Bowden leaves new tracks

It was not the way Steve Spurrier had hoped to start 1995, standing up there on the podium of the Hyatt Regency Hotel In New Orleans on the first day of the year, having to explain why he had just ditched two of his players for fighting.

Not fighting against the enemy, mind you, but fighting each other. Gator blood was shed on New Year's Eve, one player wound up in the hospital overnight and both of them were dispatched back to Gainesville as ex-Gators.

The matter of who started what and who got blamed or charged notwithstanding, the mere fact that Spurrier had to take up this time and space with such an embarrassing subject was, itself, abject humiliation for a coach.

Whether linebacker/defensive end Anthony Riggins was cut by an object or the class ring of nickel backer Darren Hambrick as the two of them wrestled on the top of a table where teammates had been dining isn't nearly as much fun to talk about as Free Shoes University.

It's New Year's Day, you're 24 hours away from your final game of the 1994 season, you're coming off a huge victory for the SEC title and two of your players grab the headlines with a bloody brawl.

'Bowden chose not to retaliate. At least for now.'

Even Bobby Bowden couldn't help but feel sympathetic toward his arch-rival. After being told about the plight of Riggins and Hambrick and asked if he'd encountered any player problems from the night before, the FSU coach offered a little levity on the matter:

"I haven't had any reports of anything yet," said Bowden. "But I ain't too anxious to look at my mail, either. If something major had occurred I would have heard. I think there could be some little minor things that the (assistant) coaches would handle.

"They're supposed to handle the minor stuff--the murders, the killings, etc. I handle those a minute late to the meeting and stuff like that."

Humor about such serious things is sometimes the best way to deflect it.

Bowden, in other words, wasn't about to gloat, because he knows just how vulnerable coaches can be when it comes to controlling the behavior of his players.

Despite Spurrier's "Free Shoes University" crack the year before, Bowden chose not to retaliate. At least for now.

To his credit, Spurrier moved swiftly on the matter of disciplining the two players for fighting.

The Gator coach doesn't deliberate when it comes time to dish out punishment. He has zero tolerance for stupidity and anti-social behavior.

Hambrick's terrific athletic ability had come to light in the win over Georgia and vaulted him into the starting lineup.

On one of the most impressive interception runbacks at Florida Field by any Gator player, offensive or defensive, Hambrick took on the persona of a Gale Sayers as he leaped over bodies and streaked down the sideline for a touchdown.

It would turn out to be the one and only highlight that Hambrick would take from his career at Florida.

The absence of either Riggins or Hambrick would not likely impact the outcome of the USF&G Sugar Bowl.

And while this game wouldn't affect the national championship, the Sugar Bowl certainly would light up a lot of TV sets around the state of Florida.

The biggest question about "The Overtime Bowl" was whether FSU's Danny Kanell could find the magic which he captured in the bottle in the final 13 minutes of that 31-31 deadlock on Nov. 26. Many wondered if Kannel's' success in the 28-point comeback could be attributed to:

a)The Gators' soft prevent defense?

b)The magic of momentum?

c)Great execution by FSU and Kanell?

The way Bowden and Kanell see it, the answer was definitely "c." But the prevailing post-mortem just after the game was played in Tallahassee five weeks ago was "a."

The Gator defenders, themselves, even lashed out at their coaches for the scheme which was rendered helpless by the FSU shotgun formation. That was in the heat of battle. In retrospect, everybody agreed the Seminoles happened upon a remedy for Florida's torrid pass rush and Kanell made it work.

"It was execution," said Bowden. "It was not motivation, or magic. And when I looked at that film after the game, I thought I was going to see a situation where Florida sat back and let us have all this short stuff and they just misjudged the time.

"That ain't what happened. They used everything they had. This dad-gum quarterback (Kanell), he just completed 'em anyway. So it's going to get down to execution, but it's not likely to happen again. If we could just get 50 per cent of what happened that last 13 minutes I'd be happy."

It's doubtful that any FSU quarterback, ever, will be able to duplicate Kanell's feat, considering that he established an NCAA record for the biggest comeback. The tipoff is that even Bowden doesn't know.

"Now, can he do it again? Well, I expect them (Florida) to give him some different looks," said Bowden.

Without admitting it, Bowden knew it wasn't likely Kanell would develop as hot as hand as he had that day back in November in Tallahassee. That would *never* happen again. Still, Bowden was propping up the confidence of his quarterback, admitting he had made a mistake in yanking him in the game the Seminoles lost to Miami.

There was a noticeable difference in the composure of the two coaches. Bowden seemed to enjoy--almost revel--in dialogue with the media. Spurrier had that pained looked, as if he couldn't wait for it to be over.

Generally, rematches don't ever live up to their billing. More times than not they become rematch/mismatches. Perhaps Steve Spurrier sensed what was coming for his Gators.

Though Florida fans had hoped to "even the score" in the USF&G Sugar Bowl, it would turn out that the closest they would come to that was when the Gators tied the Seminoles, 31-31. Or, the Seminoles tied the Gators.

Frankly, Florida would be fortunate enough to hang around long enough in the second half to make a run at FSU in New Orleans, considering the 'Noles jumped out to a 17-3 lead, scoring a record 17 points in the second quarter.

This was a measure of revenge for FSU defensive coordinator Mickey Andrews, whose defense had been riddled for 31 points the first three quarters of the Nov. 26 game.

Andrews came up with a strong defensive rushing scheme that shut down Florida's running game and blitzes which seemed to confuse pass blocking assignments. Though pressure was brought to Wuerffel, you wouldn't know it from just his numbers: A Sugar Bowl record 394 yards on 28 of 39 passes.

Big plays kept Florida in the game, including an 82-yard pass play from Wuerffel to Ike Hilliard which cut down the Seminoles' lead to 20-10 at the half.

FSU held that lead and expanded it to 23-10 with Dan Mowrey's third field goal.

Three turnovers didn't help Florida's cause. Ever so slowly, the Gators eased back into contention in the second half, though it wasn't very pretty or very early. By losing their composure over an official's questionable pass interference call, the Seminoles left the back door open.

The cagey Wuerffel sneaked through it for a touchdown after three tries from the 1-yard line. There was only 3:47 remaining, but the 'Noles' lead was trimmed to 23-17. Was there a miracle left in Spurrier's play book?

The stage was set for it as the Gators took over at their own 31 with 2:27 to play. But on second down, linebacker Todd Rebol lived up to his "big game performer" rep that the FSU press guide tagged him with.

Flashing through untouched on second down, Rebol sacked Wuerffel and seemed to rattle him. On the next play, Wuerffel was intercepted by linebacker Derrick Brooks. It ended there, FSU holding on for the 23-17 victory.

Not surprisingly, Gator-killer Warrick Dunn, from just up the road in Baton Rouge, was named MVP.

At 65, Bobby Bowden isn't too old to learn. And if there's one lesson that the veteran Florida State coach taught himself this season it's that, in a game of chance, sometimes the risk isn't worth the reward.

The two-point conversion Bowden never went for back on Nov. 26 proved a Solomon-like decision, though it may not have seemed so. Though he received a litany of criticism for kicking the extra point that only gave FSU a 31-31 tie five weeks ago, that was the only scenario which would have allowed the Seminoles to harvest Sugar Bowl gold.

Had they converted the two-pointer, the Seminoles would have wound up playing in the Cotton Bowl.

If they had gone for two and missed, they would have played Colorado in the Fiesta.

So the only scenario that would have allowed Bowden to be up there on the podium with Miller-Digby MVP winner Dunn was, indeed, the controversial choice of the 1-point conversion. A scenario, incidentally, that put more than a $1 million extra in the FSU treasury, produced an overtime and gave Bowden another chance to beat his arch rival.

"If we'd have made it (the two-point conversion)," Bowden said, "it wouldn't have made us any happier than the tie. Now Florida. . .the only way they can save face was for us to go for two and miss it. If we'd have gone for two and made it, that wouldn't have hurt them any worse than a tie.

"I gotta live with them guys 365 days a year--I wasn't going to lose that dang thing, boy. It worked out good. I've lost too many dang games going for two. You get older, you learn."

Conversely, Steve Spurrier has to "live with them guys," too. And about the only thing worse than losing to the Seminoles and hearing about it all off-season is tying them and then losing in a bowl on the final day of the season. It leaves an eight-month aftertaste.

You get older, you learn. Words of wisdom for Steve Spurrier. At a fairly youthful 49, Spurrier was yet to experience the aging process, something he is often kidded about. Someday Spurrier would discover that patience is virtue, tolerance is endearing and a touch of gray hair can be disarming. Bowden knows this. He remembers what it was like to be 49. Ten or more years ago, Bowden says, he might have lost this Sugar Bowl game.

Patience has changed him and he feels he and his coaching staff are "more settled" and "more confident" in their preparation.

"I think you are more impatient when you're young," Bowden said, without naming Spurrier's name.

"I know I certainly was. And I'm a lot more tolerant now than I was 10 years ago. . like with a kid stepping out of line. I'll talk to him a little more about it."

However, Bowden is remembering less and less what it's like to lose to Florida, because the Seminoles have dominated the series in the last nine years.

"We haven't actually dominated," said Bowden. "We've won, but it's been darn close in most cases. You get back to the bowls, and people ask us why we've won them:

"Probably because we've got better players than the people we're playing. I'm not saying we've got better players than them (Florida), we've just got a few MORE better players. But that thing will roll the other way."

The fact is that "that thing" hasn't rolled the other way now for a decade. FSU has now won 10 straight post-season games, 12 of its last 13, and finished above Florida in the final polls every year since 1985.

And, of course, Bowden is 7-1-1 against the Gators in his last nine outings and 4-1-1 against Spurrier.

Bowden is exactly right. Florida State has held a recruiting edge ever since the Gators first got into trouble with the NCAA back in the mid-eighties under Pell and Hall.

Prior to 1986, Florida held a whopping 22-7-1 advantage in the series. Getting more blue chip players out of the state has turned "that thing" around.

That doesn't detract anything from Bowden's coaching, which has been masterful.

The sly old fox with the bag of tricks has taken his young counterpart to school in recent years. Bowden also knows Spurrier is a force with which to be reckoned.

Some day historians will look back at the Bowden-Spurrier matchups as classic studies in deception. Both are masters of the illusion on offense. They often try to one-up each other in trick plays.

"I call them 'trumping'," said Bowden. "When he hit that reverse pass on us, we trumped him with that dang pass we threw (Dunn to Tiger Ellison for a 72-yard touchdown)."

By the same token, Bowden has a healthy respect for Spurrier's willingness to go Air Mail at any time. "The biggest difference between this guy (Spurrier) and anybody I've ever played is his ability to throw a bomb," said Bowden.

"Some people can't even throw a bomb. Some people can throw it, but they won't. Some people can call it sometime. This guy will call it every down if you don't watch it. Really, they can go deep as good as anybody I've ever seen."

Bowden is likely to coach until he's 70. So we'll still be treated to the Spurrier-Bowden Magic Show a few more years.

Somebody jested that there was a petition going around asking that Bowden be retired. "I wouldn't be surprised," said Bowden, playing along with the joke. "They can't wait for me to drop a couple so they can bring up that 'age thing.'"

If there was such a petition, Spurrier would be the first to sign it. Because until Bowden is sent out to pasture, it looks like the Gators may be hard pressed to win any state championships, let alone national championships.

"Spurrier will retire him," said one Alabama writer who has watched Spurrier's dominate Stallings. "He'll have his day."

Until then, however, maybe the best thing the younger Florida coach could do was follow the advice of his chief adversary: Live and learn. The learning wasn't so difficult. It was living for the next few months that was going to be tough.

Florida State's season ended on a high note, a 10-1-1 for Bowden and a No. 4 in the AP Poll and No. 4 in CNN/USA Today. Florida, at 10-2-1, was seventh in both polls. Nebraska won the national championship.

XXIII. greatest Gator player, greatest Gator coach

It was just about a year after I had made my last visit to see Steve Spurrier when I returned to his office on the Florida campus in March, 1995. About a month before Spurrier's 50th birthday, I sat down with him one final time to review his first five years in office and, in particular, the '94 season.

Though crippled and walking on one crutch after surgery to repair an old knee injury, the Gator coach was in relatively good spirits. Things were looking up. It had been a top five national recruiting class for Florida. There was already talk that Florida would be ranked as high as third in pre-season polls.

Despite problem players as well as the painful year-ending loss to FSU, Spurrier appeared upbeat and ready for the next season. Obviously the previous autumn hadn't produced the national championship everybody wanted, but it could hardly be labeled as a "down year."

All Spurrier *did* produce in 1994 was (ho-hum):

- Another win over Alabama for the SEC title;
- Sugar Bowl appearance, a fourth straight bowl;
- Fourth straight top-ten ranking at season's end;
- Best five-year record in the SEC (35-6);
- Third 10-win (or more) season (10-2-1).

'You can't take money to the grave, but you can titles and championships'
--Steve Spurrier quoting Byron Nelson

Which means Spurrier *averaged* 9.9 wins in his first five campaigns.

You know how many Gator coaches in history even achieved 10 victories in a single season just one time?

None.

The greatest football player in Florida history has become the greatest football coach in its history: So far, 49 wins, 12 losses, one tie, (.798) three SEC titles, four bowl games. And no letup in sight.

Clearly, a sound barrier has been broken.

"I wonder how the fans of Tennessee or Georgia or one of those other SEC schools would feel if their teams--somebody besides Alabama and Florida--played in the championship game," Spurrier mused..

A valid point. In the first three SEC title games there were only two participants: The Tide and the Gators. Florida won two and barely lost the other on a late interception.

In a year where Florida had three tight games, tying one (FSU), losing one (Auburn) and winning one (Alabama), Spurrier feels like his team is playing consistent enough football to compete for a national title. But he also feels to focus on that goal alone is a mistake.

Of the three close games in 1994, Spurrier feels his team won the most important one: The SEC title game with Alabama.

Not that he wouldn't have loved to have beaten Auburn and FSU, but he has his reasons.

"Of those three, we won the right one," he said. "You get a ring for that. You get your names in the record book. Byron Nelson (who once won 11 straight golf tournaments) said--and I use this quote a lot--'you can't take money to your grave, but you can take titles and championships.'

"So for the 1994 season, our guys are SEC champions forever."

Once the Gators had their first SEC title, hard core fans began to wonder what was taking him so long to win that elusive national championship.

After all, Miami and Florida State had already done it.

They must have overlooked the fact that in five short years Spurrier took a college football program out of near oblivion and thrust it into national prominence.

Spurrier looks at his team's six-week run as No. 1 rather philosophically.

The lesson about trying to be national champions, he said, could be learned from the plight of Penn State, which finished the season undefeated and wound up second to Nebraska.

"Sometimes your goals should not be to win the national championship," he said. "Penn State did everything you could ask of them and didn't win the national championship.

"How can they be a failure? That's why you hear me talk more about the SEC, because realistically if you win your division and win that game in Atlanta, that's a definite goal you have a chance to achieve.

"Sometimes too many people talk too much about winning the national championship when they should be talking about winning their conference--if they're good enough. Not to say we don't want to win it someday."

As for not keeping the No. 1 ranking after the loss to Auburn, "that's no disgrace. . .I got a feeling we'll be No. 1 again someday."

Fact is, Spurrier might have only been two plays in 1994 from his chance for a national championship trophy:

1)When Florida failed to stop Auburn on fourth down and 10 yards to go in the final minutes of the game;

2)Any one of a dozen defensive chances to stop FSU in the fourth period after taking a 31-3 lead with 13 minutes left to play in "The Choke at Doak."

The national championship scenario:

Florida beats Auburn, holding serve at No. 1, beats the Seminoles Nov. 26 and doesn't have to face them again, playing somebody like Notre Dame in the USF&G Sugar Bowl, which they would likely have beaten. Nebraska never overtakes the Gators.

Now *that's* a mythical title.

As it was, the season ended ignominiously with a 23-17 post-season loss to the Gators' bitterest rival. FSU put pressure on quarterback Danny Wuerffel and stifled Spurrier's offense for one of the few times all season. It was not a rematch made in heaven.

By now, some pain had subsided, but the fact remains Spurrier's rivals--Auburn and Florida State--got the best of him in 1994.

As for the fact that he can't seem to beat a team coached by a Bowden, Spurrier sloughs it off as a premise built up by the fans and media, but also admits it's true.

"They make too much out of the coaches," Spurrier said. "But it has happened: We haven't beaten them or Auburn the last two years, but we've beaten everybody else."

Personally, he has a high regard and affection for the venerable FSU coach.

"There's no way you can dislike Bobby Bowden," Spurrier said. "He's a wonderful person. With all the games and bowl games he's won, he'll go down in history as one of the best ever. I admire what he's done."

Although the Auburn loss was devastating, Spurrier also gave Terry Bowden's team some credit. In retrospect, Spurrier admitted that perhaps his team was too emotionally high for the Auburn game.

"Sometimes you can get too up and make a lot of errors," he said. "Defensively, that's one of the worst games we played all year. We might have been lucky to hold them to 36 (points).

"We had a lot turnovers, but got none. And we still had a chance to win it. We had the lead with a minute or so left. But we lost the game. Auburn hadn't lost too many, so it wasn't like we lost to some stiff team. I thought we were a better team, but that day we weren't.

"They out-played us and ended up out-coaching us, because they won the game. But sometimes when you lose one it might help you win another one down the line."

While the FSU and Auburn losses put a damper on the season, those losses did not detract from this five-year, quantum leap of Florida's program under Spurrier.

It's important to look at Spurrier's entire body of work since he left Duke and signed on to coach at his alma mater.

To do that, you must roll back the tape to the last day of 1989 when Spurrier arrived on campus and do a reality check about the true expectations of Florida football.

The program he took over in 1990 was not in as bad shape as everybody made it out to be, said Spurrier.

"We had a lot of good football players, especially on defense," he said.

That NCAA probationary period and the dark days on campus seem light years ago, now that the Gators are the pre-season favorites almost every year to win the SEC and compete for a national title.

Armed with the knowledge that he had learned how to win a conference championship in Durham with talent considerably under his present level, Spurrier said he was fairly confident his staff could figure out a blueprint for winning the school's first official SEC title.

So confident about that was Spurrier that he negotiated a $150,000 loan which he didn't have to pay back if his team reached that goal in his first five years.

In 1990, the Gators won a "mythical" SEC title, but weren't eligible due to NCAA probation. Then he won three in his next four seasons.

Obviously he got to keep the 150 grand.

"I didn't come in here and say I was going to do this and do that," Spurrier recalled, "but the expectations of Florida football were that we probably *wouldn't* win one my first five years."

Later, school officials altered that to read that he didn't have to pay the loan back if he stayed the entire length of the five-year contract, fearing perhaps they had placed too much emphasis on winning.

If he is nothing else, Steve Spurrier is a fine sculptor of college quarterbacks. He is able to generate from these teenage boys an acumen for driving the sleek new hi-tech machine that was once called his "Fun & Gun" offense.

His reputation as a quarterback coach non-pareil is intact, despite the Terry Dean incident.

That reputation is one reason the son of Kansas City Chiefs coach Marty Schottenheimer (Brian) is willing to ride the pine as a Gator backup.

If Miami was once "Quarterback U.," then Spurrier has turned Florida into the Harvard for field generals with a major in battlefield decisions. The Spurrier disciples tend to be less gifted physically, but strong in mental discipline and strategy.

Spurrier's quarterbacks are not automatons. Though the coach does call most of the plays, they are given the power to override that decision with an audible. They are, however, more like systems managers or jockeys than virtuosos.

They don't always come to him with pedigree, either. Spurrier dug Shane Matthews out from the rubble of a spring depth chart, where he was somewhere around fifth team--there were only five quarterbacks--and turned him into a two-time SEC Player of the Year.

Remember, Matthews was not even recruited by Spurrier, which is another testimony to his coaching ability.

Shane is the son of a Mississippi high school coach, Billy Matthews, who drove all the way down to Gainesville for Spurrier's very first scrimmage to no avail. His son, Shane, never got to play.

"When the scrimmage was over, somebody introduced me to Shane's dad," recalled Spurrier, "and so I had to apologize to him because Shane didn't even get in the scrimmage. I had four guys rotating.

"His dad said, 'Hey, I understand, you can't get 'em all in there. But I just wanted to tell you that Shane thinks he can play better than these other guys.'

"And I said, 'Really? Well, I'm going to start giving him more of a chance.'"

One candidate broke a toe. Donald Douglas transferred back to Houston. So now there were just three of them.

Magically, Matthews was transformed from the Ugly Duckling to the beautiful swan. The more heated the competition that spring, the better he played.

Pretty soon it was between Matthews and Kyle Morris, who had a big-time arm and was probably the media's favorite, but the press wasn't able to pick his No. 1 quarterback for him.

I plead guilty on that count, because I went to spring practice the first week, wrote a column about the quarterbacks and never mentioned Shane Matthews.

When they opened the 1990 season, Matthews began a three-year quarterbacking career that became one of the most illustrious in Florida football history, surpassed, perhaps, only by his Heisman-winning coach:

The SEC's all-time leader in passing yards (9,297) and touchdowns (74) and holder of 50 school records and 19 SEC marks. He finished fifth in the 1991 Heisman balloting.

So what does Spurrier see in a young quarterback that convinces him the kid can run his offense?

Not perfect mechanics.

"We work on being as good fundamentally as possible, but each player has a little bit different throwing motion.

"Just like golfers. Everybody's got their own little swing. Quarterbacks have their own little style of throwing."

Not a great arm.

"They don't have to have a *real* strong arm, but an accurate and fairly strong arm."

Not a big body. Or 4.3 time in the 40-yard dash.

It's all about good decision making.

"There's a lot of thinking. And that's something Shane was very good at. What the really top quarterbacks can do is make good decisions."

And you've got to find the open man.

"Usually when you send four or five receivers out, there's one open. And when he can find that guy and hit him and not get stuck or hung up or take a lot of sacks, he's got a chance to play very well."

Although some people charge Spurrier with keeping his quarterbacks on a short leash, the fact is that they have a great amount of authority on the field.

"We give the quarterback the freedom to change the play, try to get to a better one," said Spurrier. "The reason people think we jerk the quarterback around is because of what happened last year."

He didn't want to identify it, but you knew he was talking about the benching of Terry Dean.

"Shane Matthews played all three years. But if a quarterback is not playing well and you've got another one that's capable, then I believe you've got to give the other player an opportunity."

When Spurrier starts talking about why football coaches are such scapegoats, you can hear the evidence of scars.

"You know what's neat about reading about basketball?" he said, somewhat kiddingly but mostly serious. "Basketball players don't bitch about their coaches. Some of them do, but very seldom around here.

"And when they lose a game, the media doesn't blast the coach. They say, 'well, they didn't play very well, they didn't hit that shot, they lost the ball. . .' They don't say 'the coach is a dummy.' In football, the coach is always the dummy. (That's just) the way it is. Not just here, all over the country."

Why? Primarily, says Spurrier, it's that "you have to make a decision on every play."

Spurrier feels it's because fans think they know how to coach football.

"They see something that doesn't work and they think you should have tried something else."

Off and on for five months, I studied Spurrier in his laboratory, observing one of the keenest minds in the game.

During that time, Spurrier's emotions ran the gamut, from the emotional rush of coaching the nation's No. 1 team, to the fear that turmoil might blow up everything in his face. The actual distress over costly defeats wasn't nearly as stressful as media aggravation, player insubordination and excessive complaining by certain individuals.

Some weeks were better than others, but overall he gets an "A" for a splendid season of coaching. Sometimes his play-calling bordered on ought right wizardry (Alabama) and his inner calm seemed almost iceberg-like (Tennessee).

Other times, especially in mid-season, Spurrier appeared doomed by self-inflicted duress (Auburn), so unhappy that friends feared he hit a wall emotionally (his off-the-record press conference). Mostly what upset him was when players he perceived as selfish put themselves and their own personal accomplishments before the team.

The most important lesson Spurrier learned from 1994, he said, was that he needs to take a firmer hand in eliminating so much grousing by individuals who have their own private agenda.

All that, he says, is going to change.

"Hopefully we'll be more team-oriented in the future. I was understanding last year, but I'm going to be a little quicker to eliminate the bitching and complaining. Not from everyone, but a few. We had too much individualism. But in a way, that's our fault as coaches for allowing it.

"The part that was not fun was when we have players complaining. We had some defensive players, our quarterback (Dean), our receiver (Jackson). . .That's not very much fun. And, hopefully, we got rid of all that last year."

That, apparently, is why some of us saw a Steve Spurrier we did not know, why long-time friends and associates were concerned that he seemed under more anxiety than usual.

Now that he has reached that half-century milestone, perhaps maturity will help change that. But don't count on it.

XXIV. dancing the night away on your 50th birthday

It is 10:30 p.m. on the evening of Stephen Orr Spurrier's 50th birthday party, now 5 1/2 hours old, held on the Touchdown Terrace overlooking the north end zone of Ben Hill Griffin Stadium. Where better than Florida Field--the scene of his greatest accomplishments as a player and coach--for him to begin the second half century of his life?

This has been a grand evening, the kind you don't want to end. The last couple of dozen diehards remaining from about 175 guests are out there on the dance floor, excorising the demons in their feet. One of them is the guest of honor, Coach Spurrier--or as his friends call him, "Orr"--who has just been sufficiently toasted and roasted.

It is a dance floor full of celebrants. They have line-danced, snake-danced, bunny-hopped, twisted and jitterbugged the evening away and are showing no signs of slowing down.

Three on the dance floor are members of his family. At least two others are known, card-carrying members of the sports writing fraternity. And even more remarkably, they are laughing kibitzing as though they are having a good time together!

'Steve Spurrier is really a good guy. He just doesn't want anybody to know it.'

Heaven forbid! Spurrier is cavorting with the enemy, no less! This kind of image just doesn't go hand-in-hand with a fire-breathing, visor-flinging, quarterback-flogging coach of those big, bad Florida Gators whom everyone loves to hate.

Two of the older members of the media, obviously wiser, are sitting off to the side of the dance floor, sunken in easy chairs, lamenting the fact that somebody's camera isn't there to capture this frivolity for posterity.

"You know," said one of these sage observers of numerous Florida football campaigns, "Steve Spurrier is really a good guy. He just doesn't want anybody to know it."

Indeed, if there was underlying theme of the night that followed you home, it was that: Steve Spurrier IS a good guy.

He just needs to let more people see him relaxed like he was that night of his 50th birthday party. Or maybe he doesn't, because it would hinder his image as a villain.

For over an hour that night, Spurrier had sat listening, face on, as 18 different speakers came to the lectern to needle him. And, in a few cases, pay homage to him.

These particular brands of poison, incidentally, were chosen by the Birthday Boy himself. And though sometimes a little uncomfortable, he seemed to regale in it.

In no special order, these were some of Spurrier's vulnerable spots which were targeted:

1)That he's a tightwad of the Jack Benny genre;
2)That he is a techno-illiterate;
3)That he has mysteriously escaped the aging process;
4)That his greatest accomplishment was choosing a Florida coed named Jerri Starr to marry
5)That his competitive nature often gets the best of him.

We were all having a good time at his expense.

Did somebody say Steve Spurrier was thin-skinned?

The group included a cross-section of former teammates, former players, current assistant coaches, friends, former high school and college coaches, one former Florida president and a couple media types.

The night belonged to the Spurrier family, however, because the two liveliest speakers of the evening were Steve and Jerri's oldest son, Steve Jr., and daughter, Amy Moody.

Many comments of affection were directed toward Jerri, not just Steve. A consensus of the evening: Steve lucked out in his choice of marriage partners. We all agreed marrying Jerri was a greater achievement than winning the Heisman Trophy or SEC championship.

"When I think back to elementary school basketball, or one of his key hits in baseball, or kicking a field goal in college, or the upset of Clemson when he was at Duke, or beating Alabama at Tuscaloosa, I realize Steve has made a lot of great decisions in his life," said Lonnie Lowe of Johnson City, Tenn., Spurrier's best friend for 41 years.

"But the greatest decision he ever made was to marry Jerri," said Lowe, and then he began to choke up.

When Jerri came forward, she said briefly: "I'm like Lisa (her other daughter). I don't talk. That's how I've stayed married to Steve for nearly 30 years." And sat down.

Mike Bianchi did an imitation of Spurrier calling him early in the morning to lodge a minor complaint over choice of words in a story. "I didn't say we were GOING to win the SEC," Bianchi said, mocking the Gator coach. "I said HOPEFULLY that we MIGHT be fortunate enough to win the SEC."

Bianchi also noted that in 1945, the year Spurrier was born, the following also happened:

- Penicillin was invented
- Ballpoint pens went on sale
- White Christmas, sung by Bing Crosby, was No. 1 on the charts

■Harry Truman was president

■Hitler was killed

Sometimes Spurrier would retort playfully under his breath, other times he'd just laugh. When you can handle ribbing from family, however, that's the *real* challenge.

"Many times we have wondered," said Steve Jr.--they call him "Bubba,"-- "if dad wasn't a football coach, what exactly would he be?"

Then the younger Spurrier went on to inform the audience about his father's lack of mechanical prowess:

"One day I came home and my little brother, Scotty, 8, was explaining to my father how to use the microwave," said Steve Jr.

On another occasion, after his father's car clock went begging for two months following the Daylight Savings time change, Steve Jr. decided to move it forward an hour.

Instead of being pleased, Steve Sr. remarked: "Now I've got to remember that the clock isn't an hour off!"

Being Gator football coach isn't always easy, but this stuff of keeping up as a '90s dad can be brutal.

Daughter Amy, coming to the lectern with her notes because "dad always says that if you don't make notes, you shouldn't be allowed to speak," decided her commentary would be on her father's ability to look so young.

So she offered up "Top Seven Reasons Dad Looks So Young at 50." Among Amy's best offerings were:

"May have smoked cigarettes, but never inhaled. . .

"Maintains a low stress, high stability occupation. . .

"Delayed life cycle and didn't complete adolescence until 1978. . .

" Thick skin doesn't wrinkle.

"Just trying to keep up with older wife."

Some of the other gems that were unearthed:

■Associate Athletic Director Norm Carlson: "I beat Steve one time in golf. It was because he gave me so many strokes. When we got down to the last few holes, he said to me, 'don't you have any pride? I give Dwayne Dixon (assistant head coach) 28 strokes and he doesn't even PLAY golf!'" Carlson stood his ground and held on shamelessly for his once-in-lifetime victory. And brags about it.

■Athletic Director Jeremy Foley: "I'm the guy who has to negotiate Steve's contract. And when you have to do that every three weeks, sometimes it's not so easy."

■Jacksonville talk show host David Lamm: "Steve Spurrier picked up a check once in 1985 and again in 1993."

Some things never change, despite the years. Pulling out an old story from the *Miami Herald,* circa 1965, written by Neil Amdur, now executive sports editor of the *New York Times*, Carlson documented the fact that Spurrier's candor has always been natural to him. And often gets him in hot water.

Somewhat surreptitiously, Carlson had found a loophole that would get Spurrier elected as an Academic All-American.

"Back then," said Carlson, "they counted the grades from the semester prior. So Steve had taken a three-hour course in health and fitness the summer before and made an 'A' in it."

A reporter from the Miami Herald asked the Gators' quarterback about the scholastic honor. And what does Spurrier say? For one thing, that he wasn't all that excited about making the Academic All-American team.

(Quoting Carlson, who is quoting Amdur's article, who is quoting Spurrier's response to the *Herald*)

"I had this professor who favored football players. I think that's why he's no longer here. I really didn't study until the pressure was on."

Later, when Spurrier's comments raised the ire of some --does this sound familiar?--he amended that comment.

"Well, I really *wasn't* excited. But I didn't realize people would get so upset about what I said. I guess it's sometimes better to nod your head and be sweet about it."

Obviously, Spurrier hasn't listened to his own advice.

I suggested, as one who was already a member of the Half Century Club, that Steve learn to enjoy his second 50 by "taking a walk on the wild side--doing some things differently."

For instance:

"Throw something other than your visor-- a shoe.

"Hug a sports writer.

"Beat a Bowden."

There was a moment of silence after the last comment and maybe a groan of disapproval, but it quickly faded into the night as the merriment wafted through the evening. I heard Spurrier comment in a hushed tone: "I *have* beaten one."

Overall, this was a fine way to remember the past eight months. And a good note on which to end the story.

On the morning of my 57th birthday, after breakfast with my sister and niece, Sherri George, I closed up the house at 18 SE 14th Avenue in Ocala and loaded the car.

It was one of those spectacular lemon-lime spring days in Florida when the dappling sunshine energizes everything in your immediate universe and breathes life into your very soul.

Though still mid-morning, the mockingbird was singing heartily in the nearby oak. I made a quick inspection of my citrus trees in search of new fruit, said goodbye and turned east on State Highway 40, looking once more over my shoulder in the rear view mirror at my indomitable 57-year-old homestead. It was a comforting sight, because I knew I would be back soon and see it still standing. But for now, my work was done here, *Down Where The Old Gators Play.*

THE END

the '94 season produced 'greatest Gator game ever'

Even if they didn't realize the dream of a national championship, the 1994 Gator football season produced what some say will be the greatest win in school history in the Greatest Gator Game Ever played.

By a narrow margin, a special panel of broadcasters and writers voted Florida's 24-23 comeback victory over Alabama in the Georgia Dome on Dec. 3, 1994 as the best football game ever played in University of Florida history, edging out the 1991 Florida win over Florida State, 14-9.

That same group voted QB Steve Spurrier (1964-66) and RB Emmitt Smith (1987-89) unanimous choices for best offensive player and DE Wilber Marshall (1980-83) and DE Jack Youngblood (1968-69) unanimous as defensive players.

The vote for Greatest Gator Team ever ended in a virtual tie, with the1984 team coached first by Charley Pell and then by Galen Hall winning a "tie-breaker." The '84 Gators posted a 9-1-1 record and won Florida's first unofficial SEC title. The Steve Spurrier-coached 1991 Gators (10-2) which won Florida's first official SEC title and beat the Seminoles lost the tie-breaker and finished second.

Voting in the poll were: Tom McEwen, *Tampa Tribune*; Mike Bianchi, *Gainesville Sun*; Jack Hairston, *Gator Pipeline;* Larry Vettel, WRUF and Sports Channel; Hubert Mizell, *St. Petersburg Times;* Larry Guest, *Orlando Sentinel;* Peter Kerasotis, *Florida Today;* Frank Frangie, *Florida SportsScene and WNZS;* Dan Hincken, WTLV-TV, Jacksonville; John Oesher, *Florida Times Union;* David Lamm, WNZS; Chris Harry, *Tampa Tribune;* Keith Niebuhr, *Tallahassee Democrat;* Mike Cobb, *Lakeland Ledger;* Mark Pino, *Ocala Star-Banner;* Norm Carlson, Associate Athletic Director, Florida; Buddy Martin.

greatest Gator games

1. Florida 24, Alabama 23. 1994

2. Florida 14, Florida State 9. 1991

3. Florida 18, Auburn 17. 1986

4. Florida 59, Houston 34. 1969

5. Florida 10, Alabama 6. 1963

6. Florida 31, Florida State 31. 1994

7. Florida 18, Georgia Tech 17. 1960

8. Florida 17, Alabama 13. 1990

9. Auburn 36, Florida 33. 1994

10. (tie) Florida 27, Georgia 0. 1984
Florida 30, Auburn 27 1966
Florida 25, Kentucky 17. 1984
Georgia 26, Florida 21. 1980

greatest Gator players

OFFENSE

1. (tie) *Steve Spurrier, QB. 1964-66
*Emmitt Smith, RB. 1987-89

3. Shane Matthews, QB. .1990-91

4. Wes Chandler, WR. 1974-77

5. (tie) John L. Williams. 1982-85
Lomas Brown, OT. 1981-84

7. (tie) Cris Collinsworth, WR. 1977-80
John Reaves, QB. 1969-71

9. Neal Anderson, RB. 1982-85

10. (tie) Carlos Alvarez, WR 1969-71
Jack Jackson, WR. 1992-94
Errict Rhett, RB 1990-93

OTHERS

Larry Dupree, FB. 1962-64
Nat Moore, RB 1972-73
Larry Smith, RB 1966-68
Kerwin Bell, QB. 1984-87
Willie Jackson, WR. 1991-93
Charles Casey, WR. 1964-65
**Rick Casares, RB. 1951-53
**Chuck Hunsinger, RB 1946-49
**Dale Van Sickel, E/DE. 1927-29

DEFENSE

1. (tie) *Wilber Marshall, LB 1980-83
*Jack Youngblood, DE. 1968-70

3. (tie) Huey Richardson. 1987-90
Jarvis Williams, DB 1984-87

5. Scot Brantley, LB. 1976-79

6. Alonzo Johnson, LB. 1981-85

7. (tie) Kevin Carter, DE. 1991-94
Louis Oliver, DB. 1984-88

8. (tie) Ralph Ortega, LB
Glenn Cameron, LB 1972-74

10. David Little, LB 1977-80

OTHERS

Steve Tannen, DB. 1967-69
Brad Culpepper, DL 1988-91
**Charles LaPradd, OT/DT 1950-52
**Vel Heckman, DT 1956-58

KICKERS

**Bobby Raymond, placekicker. 1983-84
**Judd Davis, placekicker. 1992-94

PUNTERS

**Don Chandler. 1954-55
**Bobby Joe Green 1958-59

*unanimous **author's choice

greatest Gator teams

Team	Record	Coach
1. 1984	9-1-1	Charley Pell/Galen Hall
2. 1991	10-2	Steve Spurrier
3. (tie) 1993	11-2	Steve Spurrier
1994	10-2-1	Steve Spurrier
5. 1985	9-1-1	Galen Hall
6. 1969	9-1-1	Ray Graves
7. 1983	9-2-1	Charley Pell
8. 1990	9-2	Steve Spurrier
9. 1966	9-2	Ray Graves
**10. 1928	8-1	Charles Bachman

**author's choice

about the author

W.F. Buddy Martin is a former sports editor/columnist of four Florida newspapers who began following the Florida Gators in the early 1950s and covered them as a sports columnist for more than a dozen years.

Martin's newspaper career started at the *Ocala Star-Banner*, where both his father, Wilton Martin, and grandfather, William Laban Martin, also began their journalism careers.

Down Where The Old Gators Play is his fourth book. Although most of Martin's background is in newspapers-- he has served as sports editor of such metro dailies as *The New York Daily News, The Denver Post* and *The St. Petersburg Times*--he most recently worked in network TV as editorial consultant for CBS Sports.

At CBS as an associate producer, Martin was awarded an Emmy for his work on *The NFL Today*, where he produced segments for analyst Terry Bradshaw from 1990 through 1992 under producer Eric Mann.

Martin is the media director of *The Sprint INTERNATIONAL* golf tournament at Castle Pines and a Denver TV talk show host. This is his fourth book.

Buddy's other books include: *Looking Deep,* the 1991 autobiography of Hall of Fame quarterback Terry Bradshaw; *Parting Shots,* the autobiography of former Nuggets player and coach Dan Issel; *That Super Season,* the Denver Broncos' drive to the Super Bowl.

Martin was born and raised in Ocala, Florida and attended journalism school at the University of Florida. He is married to the former Joan Sharp of North Miami. All three of their children were born in Florida: Lori Martin (Ocala) of Waterton, Massachusetts; Rebecca Martin (Cocoa Beach) and Brenden Martin (St. Petersburg) of Littleton, Colorado. Buddy and Joni reside in both Littleton and Ocala.

acknowledgments

There are dozens to thank for taking this leap of faith with me. Members of my family, especially, assisted in so many ways, especially my wife, Joni, who believed in this book and granted me a temporary reprieve of chores, but reminds me that I am no longer exempt from lawn-mowing duties.

One of the true joys of this assignment was the privilege of spending time with my sister, Shirley Lovell, a Gator fanatic, who supported me in every way imaginable and was my traveling mate for all the games. Shirley also made it possible for me to move back into the house in which we grew up.

My mother-in-law, Lori Byrd of Boca Raton, who collects furniture the way some people collect coins, generously furnished the Ocala house so that I was able to headquarter there. Her husband, John, kept it all working.

Having capable editors in the family always helps. And that came from Joni, Lori Martin, Rebecca Martin, Brenden Martin and Scott Hossfeld. My good friend Walt Tomooka and associate Cindy Zoetewey also excelled as proof readers.

The diligent watch as my extra set of "eyes and ears" when I had to be away from Florida were provided by Augie Greiner and Scott Lovell. My niece, Sherri George, and her husband, Howard, took care of videotaping the games.

There were many others, including Frank Frangie, David Lamm, Jack Hairston and Mike Bianchi. Hairston and Frangie pored over the manuscript, offering key suggestions which illuminated the text with perspective. Friend Neil Amdur of the *New York Times* always encouraged me.

And if Bart and Miriam Kimball hadn't conspired with Reed Brown to have me speak to the Gainesville Quarterback Club, this whole idea might not have evolved.

So many people to thank, such little space:

Thank You!

Robbie Andreu	Brad Lucas & Lori Martin
Lori & John Byrd	Brenden & Joan Martin
Mike Bianchi	Scott Hossfeld & Rebecca Martin
Irv Brown	Don & Martha Meyers
Ken Brown	Hubert Mizell
Reed Brown	Ed & Marsha Monarchik
Norm Carlson	Gene Peek III
Frank Frangie	Charlotte & Carswell Ponder
Sherri & Howard George	Jonna Santangelo
Augie & Susan Greiner	Jerri & Steve Spurrier
Jack Hairston	Bill Taaffe
John Humenik	Larry Thiel
Pete Kerasotis	Walt Tomooka
Bart & Miriam Kimball	Rhonda & Tommy Vickers
David Lamm	Jerry Walters
Leonard Levy	Shari Wenk
Shirley Lovell	Joe Williams
Tom McEwen	Cindy Zoetewey

Plus the entire Media Panel for "Gator Greatest"

And for the gifts of: Chuck Hunsinger, The Voice of Otis Boggs, Daddy's Zenith Radio, Mother's House, Big Sister's Advice, Nana's Furniture, The Mockingbird in The Oak, The Train Whistle and the company of Faithful Black Lab Jordan.

For additional copies or information on this book call
Kendall/Hunt Publishing Company: **1-800-228-0810**
Or to reach W.F. Buddy Martin call: **1-303-798-8163**